The Heart of a Warrior

The Life of Ernest Leroy Webb

By
Robert C. Carroll • James R. Ellis • John H. Fagan

ISBN 978-1-964143-03-3

Suncoast Digital Press, Inc.
Sarasota, Florida

Printed in the United States of America

Cover design: Ketti Harrison
Personal photos are courtesy of the family of Ernest L. Webb

Lieutenant Colonel Ernest Leroy Webb,
US Army (Retired)

Ernest Leroy Webb is a great patriot, a phenomenal leader, and a dear friend. But most of all, he is a warrior… a **warrior** with a **heart**.

These seemingly contradictory two words are, in fact, complementary.

- Webb is a combat hero, brave beyond the pale. He is a ferocious fighter and fearless leader. He is a **warrior** in the spiritual sense of fighting for good against evil.
- At the same time, he possesses great compassion for mankind, including the enemy he has been ordered to fight. He is extremely passionate about his country, his fellow soldiers, and his family. He has a heart for humanity.

This book is written for anyone who ever knew Ernie Webb and anyone wishing to read the biography of an amazing leader. Military history buffs will enjoy the many true accounts, including stories from West Point and the Vietnam War.

Ernie Webb, clutching Old Glory to his heart. (2021)

The Dream Team:

2d Battalion Advisory Team,
Vietnamese Airborne Division

Barry McCaffrey, Ernie Webb, Frenchy Girard

Dedication

This book is dedicated to
all the American soldiers
who died in the Republic of Vietnam.

especially

Sergeant First Class Christian G. "Frenchy" Girard,
who saved Captain Webb's life and was later killed.

Sergeant Girard's awards included three Silver Stars,
Five Bronze Stars, and Three Purple Hearts.

Contents

Dedication iv

Preface vii

Chapter 1   The Making of a Warrior 1

Chapter 2   Be All You Can Be 11

Chapter 3   Webb Enters West Point 23

Chapter 4   At War With "The System" 31

Chapter 5   The "One and Only" 41

Chapter 6   Lieutenant (Ranger) Webb 49

Chapter 7   Captain Webb Advising the Vietnamese Airborne 61

Chapter 8   Major Webb: A Warrior Goes to War 69

Chapter 9   A Warrior with a Pen 81

Chapter 10 Lieutenant Colonel Webb: Battalion Command 91

Chapter 11 The Warrior Goes Civilian 99

Chapter 12 Parade Rest 109

About the Authors 119

Appendix   How to Use QR Codes 120

Preface

By Bob Carroll

This is a biography of Ernest Leroy Webb.

The best way to introduce Ernie is to let him tell you a story from his days in Vietnam.

*　　*　　*

"A woman came out of a hut screaming in Vietnamese, 'You didn't get them all! There's one in that tunnel, and he's got my baby!'

I went over to the tunnel and yelled down in my best pidgin Vietnamese: '*Chiêu Hồi!* Surrender. Nobody will mistreat you.'

His response was the Vietnamese version of 'Go…yourself.'

'Now listen, you're gonna die if you don't give up.'

Again, 'Go … yourself.'

'Don't let this baby be part of our fight. He has nothing to do with this. You and me: One of us is going to die. But this baby doesn't have to.'

Lo and behold, this blanket comes out of the hole, with the baby in it.

I grabbed the baby, handed it to somebody, and said, 'Give this to the mother.'

That's probably the proudest moment of my life.

I went back to the guy and said, 'OK, you need to *Chiêu Hồi.*'

No response.

I threw a grenade down the hole. But the tunnel, as you know, goes back, and bends around corners. I was hoping I would at least shock him with a concussion.

As soon as the grenade went off, I dove into the tunnel and stayed very low to the ground.

The VC fired first.

Because I was low, he missed with all his shots, and I hit him with one of mine.

…I wish I hadn't had to kill him.

…But I am so thrilled…that the little baby lived.

…And the mothers in the village were so grateful, they showed us where the huts had been booby-trapped, which allowed us to complete the operation with no friendly casualties.

I'd really like to know what happened to that baby. I only wish I could see that little baby again, even after sixty years."

*　　*　　*

The above story exemplifies why we titled this book "The Heart of a Warrior."

In 2022, mutual friends Jim Ellis, Jack Fagan, and I exchanged similar stories we had heard from Ernie and about Ernie. Having observed him in a multitude of leadership positions and challenges for sixty-six years, we all marveled at the life he has led.

We asked several friends if they had stories about Ernie. The response was overwhelming. The stories cut across the board, in and out of combat, and throughout his lifetime.

As a team, we decided to compile a series of stories fashioned into chapters to portray the life of Ernie Webb.

*　　*　　*

I first met Webb on July 1, 1958, the day we both arrived at West Point. We were assigned to Company A2, one of the 24 hundred-man companies in the Corps of Cadets. After graduation in 1962, Webb and I served together in the US, Vietnam, Germany, and on the faculty at West Point. After retiring from the Army, we joined forces in teaching corporate executives the fundamentals of leadership.

Jack Fagan also started a lifelong friendship with Webb as a plebe in Company A2. A hard-working student, Jack was an outstanding academic coach for us all. He graduated first in the Class of 1962.

Jim Ellis also joined the Corps of Cadets in 1958, but he had met Webb a year earlier at the West Point Prep School. As First Captain and Brigade Commander, Jim was the top leader in the Class of 1962.

Jim recalls that in Prep School, Webb was called by his middle name, "Leroy," but at West Point, some cadets started calling him "Ernie." The moniker question was resolved during our "Firstie" (senior) year by none other than Pat Gilmore, his future wife. It has been "Ernie" ever since, but you'll find the era-appropriate name used in the stories that follow.

*   *   *

The three of us interviewed Ernie extensively to clarify facts and dates.

Additionally, we drew from a book written by his boss in Vietnam, Anthony B. Herbert: *Soldier* (New York: Holt, Rinehart, and Winston, 1973).

We also discovered an interview of Webb hosted on the Library of Congress website. As part of The Veterans History Project, a one-and-a-half-hour interview with Webb was conducted on June 10, 2019, by Joseph L. Galloway, coauthor of *We Were Soldiers Once... and Young*. This video interview is a treasure trove of stories, told in first-person by the man we pay tribute to in this book.

We coauthors are very aware that we cannot convey the true passion of our good friend with just the written word. Therefore, throughout the book, we are pleased to offer eleven short video clips (1-3 minutes each) from the above interview where you can see and hear Ernie himself. These short clips are hosted on a special YouTube channel, easily accessible using QR (Quick Response) codes, the square images placed throughout this book. If you are unfamiliar with using QR codes, please see the detailed instructions in the Appendix of this book.

As you read the book, we strongly encourage you to click on these short clips to see, hear, and appreciate the man and his stories from that era. For starters, with your smartphone, scan the QR code in the note on the following page. In just a few seconds you will hear and see Ernie relating his story of saving a Vietnamese baby.[1]

We greatly appreciate the invaluable assistance of Ernie's daughter, Maureen Webb Thorsen, and mutual friends Tom Simcox, Sammy Steele, Lewis Higinbotham, Pat Canary, Don Snider, Stan Russell, Don Kennedy, Dennis Almena, and Kathleen Carroll. Our editor Barbara Dee was extremely helpful in making these three old soldiers write with clarity and proper syntax.

Thank you all.

And thank you Ernie.

Bob Carroll

Charleston SC
July 4, 2024

---

[1]Ernie talks about the proudest day of his life. Follow the QR code to view a 2-minute segment.

Or, visit the YouTube channel below and select video #1. https://www.youtube.com/@the-heart-of-a-warrior.

Chapter 1

The Making of a Warrior

Stillwater, Oklahoma, was in rough shape during the 1930s. The Dust Bowl had closed many of the farms, driving people into the city to find work. There wasn't much of that available during the Depression. The New Deal, with its welfare and employment programs, was a late arrival due to local conservative politics. But by mid-decade, the Works Progress Administration and the Civil Conservation Corps set up shop and were making an impact when Ernest Leroy Webb was born on March 12, 1937.

Ernie was the first of four children, named after his father, a construction worker who had recently married Juanita, a local waitress. Even though money was tight, Ernie has fond memories and describes those early Oklahoma years as "delightful." His sister Irene arrived a couple of years after her brother, followed by two little brothers, Michael and Bob.

Kids in Hardscrabble Oklahoma

The family lived next door to a ranch and as soon as he started wearing long pants, Ernie did his part for the family budget by wrangling cows. "My job was to bring in the cows and milk the first three." He was 8 years old.

By then, Stillwater was a boomtown. The town fathers had converted the local college, Oklahoma A&M, into a training center for soldiers, sailors, and airmen during WWII. About 40,000 of them passed through, which translated into a lot of construction work jobs during and after the war. Stillwater was morphing from a sleepy cow town into a busy city.

Just before Ernie turned 10 years old, Juanita decided to retire from waiting tables, broke off from Webb Sr., and married Bill Maugham, a US Navy Chief Petty Officer. Soon after, the Navy detailed Maugham to Port Lyautey, a Naval Air Station in Morocco, about 75 miles northeast of Casablanca. So, Juanita and her entire brood joined her new husband in faraway North Africa.

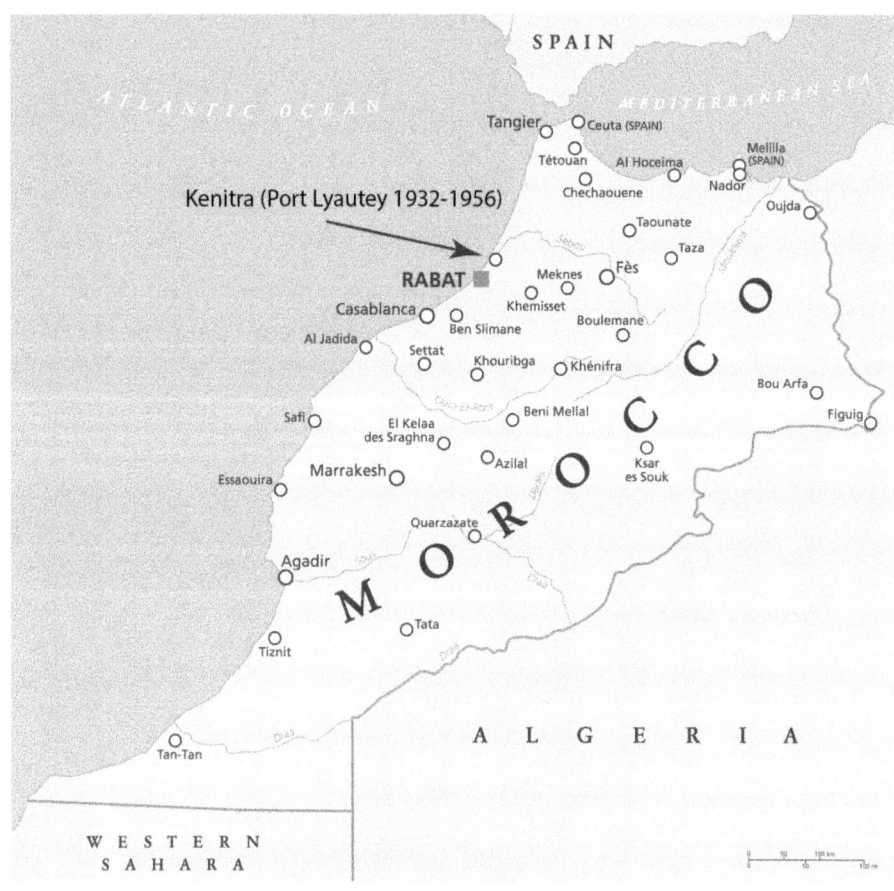

The Kingdom of Morocco

The US Navy had captured Port Lyautey from the Vichy French to establish an Advanced Landing Ground for Operation Torch back in 1942. The base hadn't changed much in five years, maintaining its WWII role as a base for US Navy Antisubmarine patrols over the Straits of Gibraltar and the western Mediterranean. It was a small outpost, without the amenities of a full-fledged Naval Air Station.

The Navy had to import a schoolteacher for the K-8 kids on the base. Then there was the off-post neighborhood. Ernie remembers that the locals were very poor: "If you dropped a coin on the ground, there would be a rush to pick it up." That kind of poverty breeds desperation—Ernie had seen some of that in Oklahoma, but nothing like this.

Dad was mostly on duty, so it was up to Mom, Ernie, sister Irene and the two little boys to adapt as best they could to life in this strange land. Ernie remembers Juanita from those days: "She was tough, maybe even a little nasty, and didn't tolerate any bullshit from anyone. That was important in Morocco."

When Dad was on patrol, Ernie was the Man of the House—in the 4th grade. His first instinct was to protect the younger kids. "Don't mess with my family!" He was especially a guardian for 8-year-old Irene. "There were lots of bums around." With bad intentions, no doubt. Out of necessity, Ernie learned to fight. There arose many opportunities to protect the family during that time, instilling a "put-up-your-dukes" mentality, which stayed with Ernie for his entire life. He has been protecting an ever-extending family ever since those years in Morocco.

After CPO Maugham's two-year hitch at Port Lyautey, the family returned to Stillwater. Ernie's memory of that time is a bit hazy but, according to daughter Maureen, "Juanita kind of gave up on the family." She parked the kids in an orphanage for a while until she could sort things out. Twelve-year-old Ernie wasn't going to stand for that and demanded that he "go to California to live with my real Dad." His mother agreed but wouldn't release the other kids from the orphanage. That was very hard for Ernie, feeling especially bad for Irene, who was having a tough time with Mom. Ernie couldn't protect her and his little brothers anymore, but he felt he had to go. That departure has haunted Ernie ever since. Later in life, he tearfully told a friend, "I still can't get over my mother giving us up for adoption."

Ernie learned some tough lessons in those early years, instilling basic principles that he never abandoned. First and foremost, protect your family in all situations. He had grown up in a broken family and always longed for a stable family environment. "Home? That's wherever the bed was!" Ernie's bed was sometimes at Juanita's place, sometimes at this or that grandparent's home. It was the same for all the Webb kids, until they all wound up at the orphanage.

Because of that upbringing, Ernie prized family life above all else. At West Point, he appreciated being included in surrogate families from among his classmates to make up for what he had missed as a child. For example, the family of classmate Jim Ellis welcomed Ernie to their home in Alabama on several occasions. Also, Sammy Steele, from Tennessee, brought Ernie home with him after a class trip.

Ernie also learned at a very young age that he had to protect his family in order to preserve it. Later, that need to protect his family extended to those who needed it most, who might have become helpless or overtaken by events. The seeds that grew into a "Warrior with a Heart" were sown when Ernie was still in grade school—strength along with compassion; a valiant yet kind soul.

Another life lesson that emerged from those early years led to Ernie's resolve to not allow others to define him. "Don't pre-judge me!" He had been judged unfavorably many times in his young life and was determined that he "wasn't ever again going to put up with any of that bullshit." Ernie himself applied that lesson whenever he encountered a new situation, especially with people who were very different from him. He was about to encounter such a situation as he set off to California to reunite with his father.

Ernie Webb Sr. had settled in Newhall, California, a Los Angeles suburb just north of the San Fernando Valley. He had married a woman who Ernie describes as "nice, quiet, and easy-going, almost an opposite of Mom." She had two little boys of her own so to avoid any confusion around the house, Ernie started using his middle name. He would be "Leroy" from now on. In the early 50s, the LA suburban sprawl hadn't reached Newhall yet, and there was extensive farming in the local area. Ernie (aka Leroy) settled in nicely, even finding part-time work at a farm near his new home. He was back wrangling cattle, milking cows, etc., just as he had done years before as a boy in Oklahoma.

High school was another matter. As a freshman new kid, "They really didn't like me at first." Even in bucolic Newhall, there were "lots of gangs" that bullied the rest of the kids. So, the gangsters started in on this Leroy Webb guy, and the other kids joined right in because they were afraid not to.

Leroy's Morocco experiences came in handy right away. He quickly identified the ringleaders and pushed back hard on the bullying, "No one gets in my way!" That took several fistfights: "I had to straighten them out." Gradually, the other kids began to realize that this new kid wasn't going to be pushed around and that he would actually stand up for them against the bullies. He was protecting a family again, just as he had done in Morocco.

When Leroy started playing sports, everything fell into place. By his sophomore year, he had made 1st team in football as "a kind of small running back."

Leroy Webb, right halfback and Co-Captain

The running continued in track, where he starred in the 100-yard dash and low hurdles. He always pushed himself to "beat the odds," at one time crossing the finish line ahead of a local State Champ "in either the 100 or the hurdles, I can't really remember." Hart High School archival photos show both events.

Leroy Webb finishes the 100-yard dash behind teammate Bob Jones, whose time was 10.1 seconds.

Leroy Webb wins the 180 low hurdles.

Leroy wasn't ignoring the books either. He had set his sights on Student Government, trading on his athletic talent and his reputation for "standing up for the little guy." To qualify for office, one had to maintain good grades, which he did. By his senior year, Webb was both Captain of the football team and Student Body President. Here, he is gaveling the class assembly to order.

Student Body President Leroy Webb

Leroy was always sensitive about the fact that he really was "a little guy." Hart High School's Varsity Club photo shows stark evidence—that's him in the middle, a full head shorter than several of his teammates.

Leroy Webb in center of Varsity Club

His short stature bothered Leroy his entire life. He would occasionally break into tears in frustration that he couldn't do anything about it. But he could compensate (and did) by "being tougher than anyone else." He displayed that toughness time and again, backing it up by fistfights whenever he felt threatened. He didn't know it then, but that fearless readiness to "put up your dukes" laid the groundwork for his lifelong warrior attitude.

Leroy hadn't thought much about pursuing college after high school. There wasn't a lot of encouragement at home nor the money to support higher education. His stepmom was ambivalent because she was hoping that Leroy would continue to be around to provide an example for her own kids, who were starting to have some trouble at school. Nevertheless, both Dad and his wife said, "It's your life…you should try to find your own way."

Leroy didn't know how to take the next steps, but a couple of his high school friends did. They set up interviews for him at Occidental College, a highly-regarded liberal arts institution about 30 miles south in Los Angeles. Leroy's high school sports record, good grades, plus his Student Government credentials earned him a one-year scholarship at Occidental. He was on his way, or so he thought.

Occidental College, Los Angeles, California

It was 1955 and Leroy had settled in nicely at Occidental, multi-tasking the academics, the daily commute, and sports. But after a while, he encountered a familiar situation. The upperclassmen on the track team were in the habit of bullying kids who, in their view, didn't measure up to team standards. The fact that they were "smart-ass rich kids" picking on scholarship types like Leroy was too much for him to take. Just as he had done in Morocco and in Newhall, he took a stand to "defend the kid who was being bullied."

In reminiscing, Leroy is a little hazy about what happened next, but, "I remember the fights." Apparently more than one. The Occidental authorities took note of the fisticuffs as well and pulled his scholarship after that first year. As far as he can recall, Leroy didn't really try to justify his actions to save his scholarship. This was just another situation that he found himself in, where he had to take action, and fast. He had depended completely on that scholarship. "There wasn't a lot of money. I cut costs by living at home, but not enough to get by without it." What now?

During his year at Occidental, looking for ways to earn money, Leroy had encountered an Army recruiter, who explained the benefits of the guaranteed job, challenging work, interesting travel…the entire "Be All You Can Be" bit, circa 1955. The recruiter also noted Leroy's determination to prove how tough he was. He told him: "The toughest guys that I know in this man's Army are the paratroopers. I can sign you up for Airborne training right after you complete Basic. How does that sound?" It sounded terrific. Leroy signed the papers and never looked back; "You're in the Army now!"

Leroy never reflected much on his decision to join the Army. He didn't lay out all the options, write out the Pros and Cons, seek expert advice, identify alternatives—no Cost/Benefit Analysis stuff. He *just did it*. He felt that he had to do something, and do it fast, just as he always had done. His actions have always been guided by gut instincts: stand up for yourself and others, never back down, and do the right thing (and do it now). He would sometimes wonder, "Damn, did I just do that?" But once a decision was made, he moved on to the follow-through. Leroy developed that approach as a young boy and has carried it out through his entire life.

Leroy would be the first to tell you that his approach to decision-making doesn't always yield ideal results. Maybe there's an element of "Ready, Fire, Aim" in there? Perhaps. But, in rapidly developing situations where there's not much time to stop and think (the battlefield maybe?), it helps to have good instincts and intentions to guide you. Besides, Leroy would also probably tell you that he couldn't do it any other way.

The Warrior with a Heart was in the making.

Chapter 2

Be All You Can Be

The US Army in the 1950s was being pulled apart by three new warfare concepts:

- Reorganization
- Mutual Security
- Demobilization

(Noted in the article, "The Army Before Vietnam, 1953 – 1965"; Carter, Donald; Center for Military History, Pub 76-3, 2015.)

Reorganization meant that the Army was subsidiary to the Navy and Air Force, developing tactics for the Nuclear Battlefield, while the other guys dealt with the strategic threat. Mutual Security meant that the Army's primary mission was now to provide weapons, equipment, and training to build local defenses in Germany, Japan, and Korea. Finally, there was Demobilization. The Army was expected to do all this with fewer troops. By 1960, the US Army headcount was down by over 80% relative to the end of the Korean War (1953).

Then, to top it off, the Army decided to ditch the traditional light brown and tan uniform (nicknamed "Pinks and Greens") and switched to black footwear from the time-honored brown shoe. So, what was your local US Army Recruiter supposed to do?

Mutual Security was the key. You didn't have to "Join The Navy To See The World." This Army gig was even better; you would LIVE in many different areas of the world. Navy swabbies might get a Port Call every couple of months, when they could go ashore to drink all day and night, enjoy the local ladies, then ship out with a 3-day hangover. But Army grunts could take their time, get immersed in the local culture, and learn about new ways to get mellow, not just wasted. This allowed for true R&R (rest and relaxation) alongside their duties. They might even get something going with exotic women who didn't look anything like the girls back home in the US. In Germany, that meant Biergartens and Frauleins; in Japan, Sake and Geisha Girls. And in Korea? Well, in Korea there was always Kimchi.

Leroy wasn't affected by any of those enticements in 1956. He had run out of options at Occidental College, and the Army was his next best meal ticket. Before he learned all about Army life in Europe, he had to survive Basic Training. So off to Fort Bragg (now Fort Liberty) he went.

Army Basic Training in the 1950s was nine weeks long. Every new enlistee went through the same four-part program regardless of where they trained, or where they would be assigned:

- Drill and ceremonies
- Physical training
- Setting up and maintaining a campsite
- Rifle marksmanship

Drill taught the enlistees how to stand at attention, give a hand salute, march, perform right face/left face/about-face, and so forth. After interminable repetition, these basic actions became second nature. The recruits also learned how to properly wear and care for the uniform (by getting chewed out every time they did it wrong). All of the training came together when they were *on parade*, which was often.

Marching

Physical training began as soon as the recruits got off the bus. The Daily Dozen: pushups, sit-ups, pull-ups, running, and other cardio-strengthening exercises prepared them for frequent long marches to nowhere. This was now their day-to-day routine.

Once the recruits became familiar with barracks life, it was time to go camping. Unlike those sing-along trips to the local State Park with Mom and Dad, brothers and sisters, this was serious stuff. They're out there in the boondocks for 10 days or more, remote from civilization, learning how to set up and maintain a campsite, prepare meals, and apply emergency first aid. And they were required to keep themselves and their gear inspection-ready clean. Sleep, for the few hours allowed, was caught by crashing out with a buddy in a two-man pup tent after an exhausting day in the field. Leroy loved it. He'd been an outdoorsy kid all his life, and this was just plain fun to him.

Rifle marksmanship was the key to Basic Training. To graduate, a soldier had to pass the PT test (measuring physical ability and stamina) and qualify in marksmanship, using the WWII M1 Garand rifle. Qualification levels were Marksman, Sharpshooter, and Expert. The target was at a distance of 100 yards and hitting the bullseye was 5 points. Each soldier would fire 50 rounds; 250 was a perfect score. *Marksmanship* was 150, *Sharpshooter* was 180, and *Expert* was 215. There were 1000 trainees in a typical battalion—four companies with four platoons each, with 60 to 65 soldiers in each platoon. Less than 5% of all trainees would qualify as *Expert*. At the graduation ceremony, the Post Commanding General would present the Expert Marksmanship Badge to those who qualified. Leroy Webb was among the esteemed five percent. "The rifle range was easy for me," Webb recalls, "No problem for an Oklahoma kid used to picking off tin cans and prairie dogs. Those KD [known distance] range targets don't move much."

On the rifle range

The new recruits learned early on that the Regular Army was no party. The NCO cadre made that very clear, by in-your-face indoctrination. As appointed non-commissioned officers, these guys were WWII and Korean War vets who had seen it all. They had one clear and compelling message: "We were surprised both times in those wars and lost a lot of friends because of it. That's not going to happen again. So, you pukes are going to get fit, you're going to learn to shoot, and I'll be all over your ass until you do!" That was what Basic Training was really all about: PT and Marksmanship. Leroy was in the top 2% in one, and in the top 5% in the latter.

The enthusiastic and creative recruiting done by the Army in the 50s brought in all kinds of characters, ranging from juvenile delinquents to college dropouts, including kids who just didn't have the means to do anything else. It was up to the Army Qualification Test to sort all that out. Your AQT Score revealed what you were really good at, and high scorers were a prized commodity.

The Army was still struggling with Reorganization, Mutual Security, and the technical challenges of developing new weapons and tactics for the emerging nuclear battlefield. Demobilization had stretched resources very thin, so there was intense competition to fill the ranks with the Best and Brightest. That process started right after Basic with Advanced Individual Training (AIT).

Leroy moved to Infantry AIT—another nine weeks of training, at Fort Jackson, South Carolina, this time. The primary focus was learning how to function as a member of a team while facing many different types of combat challenges. The best trainees would be identified as future leaders. Leroy stood out in AIT, just as he had in Basic Training. That gave him first crack at what he was aiming to become: a Paratrooper. He volunteered for Airborne training and was transferred back to Fort Bragg (now Fort Liberty) to earn his "jump wings." While at Bragg he got an Airborne tattoo on his forearm—a source of pride and also some future trouble. After a short time at Bragg (where some of that trouble started), Leroy was transferred to the 11th Airborne Division in Germany.

He didn't know it, but Leroy was being swept up in the Army's new plan to replenish the Officer Corps. During the mid-50s, the Army realized that filling the officer ranks with repurposed NCOs wasn't working. These troops had served nobly in WWII and Korea, were happy enough to stick around in the Army for their 20-year retirement, but weren't very excited about the "new look" challenges that were being thrust on them. "The ranks of field-grade officers contained some men who had been passed over for promotion, and that was contributing to the Army's difficulty in retaining good junior officers, for no one 'wants to work for a lazy, ne'er do well.' Careerism, rather than dynamism, seemed to be the watchword of the peacetime Army." (Carter, op.cit.)

"Airborne"

Why not sift through all these new recruits, figure out who has *the right stuff* to lead troops, and train them to be officers? So, in 1957, the call went out to all Army units to find qualified candidates for West Point.

Leroy always has a good laugh when he recounts how he became a West Point Cadet. "I was full of beans after I pinned on those jump wings. After all that training—Basic, AIT, Jump School—I finally had some time on my hands. The 82nd Airborne wasn't scheduled for any deployments, and barracks life was kinda boring. So, I'd spice things up by hanging out in bars, looking for fights. Especially with Marines. They were just like me, trying to prove how tough they were. I'd just say something stupid, the 'jarhead' would respond, and we'd go from there. It was either a fight, or I'd found a new drinking buddy."

Leroy must have collected a few Article 15s along the way because his Chain of Command was not amused by this new attitude. (Article 15 refers to being reprimanded for minor offenses, does not include the process of a court-martial, and results in punishments such as additional duties, fines, or restrictions.) Weary of his role of frequent disciplinarian, his 1st Sergeant put him on a transfer list to the 11th Airborne Division in Germany. "You've been a real pain-in-the-ass for me, so I'm more than happy to ship you the hell out of here. Those guys in the 11th Airborne can deal with your shit from now on."

But Fate intervened. Leroy remembers: "It was Captain Somebody-or-other, I didn't even know the guy. Out of the blue, he kind of orders me to take the qualifying exam for West Point. He must have had a quota or something."

Leroy had no intention of doing that. He told that captain that he was going to quit the Army as soon as his hitch was up.

The captain sweetened the offer. "Just take the damned exam. I'll give you three days to prepare, then throw in a three-day pass after you do it."

Deal.

Typical for the Army, it took months to process the qualifying test results for all those recruits scattered over Army posts all over the US. By then, Leroy's transfer to the 11th Airborne came through and he was in the Federal Republic of Germany. And still getting into trouble—in two languages now. But before he wore out his welcome with his new Chain of Command, new orders arrived: "Report to the West Point Military Academy Preparatory School at Fort Belvoir VA."

Leroy often reflects on that turning point in his life. "Sometimes, something comes along to settle you down." He knew that he had been messing things up with all the drinking and fighting. Maybe it was time to get serious about straightening out his life. It wasn't the first time, and wouldn't be the last, that "something" happened to put Leroy on a new and better track.

The US Military Academy Preparatory School (USMAPS) was founded in 1946 at Stewart Army Air Field in Newburgh, New York, replacing prep schools established in each of the nine Army Corps Areas in the US. In 1957, when all units were ordered to identify prospective West Point candidates, USMAPS was relocated to Fort Belvoir, Virginia, to accommodate the increased enrollment. The move closer to Washington, DC, would give candidates access to their home state representatives to apply for an Academy appointment. And it worked for several.

Private First Class Leroy Webb

The prep school was housed in an old World War II wooden, single-story hospital. The cadet company had about 200 candidates divided into five platoons. Each platoon had two barracks with 20 candidates in each. Webb had been selected for the Prep School from his Airborne Unit in Germany and was one of the first to arrive. He was assigned to the First Platoon, whose leader was a soldier named Glen Blumhardt. Shortly after Webb, Jim Ellis arrived and was told to report to the First Platoon. Platoon leader Blumhardt took Ellis to a bunk next to Cadet Candidate Ernest Leroy Webb. In the first 30 seconds, Leroy met two guys who would be at the top of his friends' list for over 60 years. They didn't know it then, but a significant chunk of the leadership of West Point Class of 1962 would emerge from those run-down barracks at Belvoir.

Compared to what these soldiers had experienced in their Regular Army units, Prep School was easy duty. The schedule was:

- Sunday
    - 1630: supper assembly
    - 1800 – 2000: study hall
    - 2200: lights out
- Monday through Friday:
    - AM academics
    - PM athletics and physical training (PT)
    - Friday: release for the weekend

Leadership training was embedded in the curriculum. The Chain of Command was similar to that of the Regular Army and to the Corps of Cadets. Everyone had a job to do and was evaluated on performance, just as in the Regular Army. It all fell into place and quickly became routine. In the First Platoon, Blumhardt needed an NCO to schedule the athletic events and PT. He appointed Leroy Webb, the guy who was already a standout performer in both areas. Good choice.

Webb, on left, with other platoon athletic NCO's

Leroy was excelling at all the physical challenges, just as he always had done. But, for the first time since high school, he was the guy LEADING the drills, up front and visible to everyone. Leroy was a natural. He could do all of the Army Daily Dozen as well as anyone, while counting out the cadence at high volume in a booming command voice. Leroy would always throw in a few jokes, maybe poke fun at a few laggards in the ranks, all with a good-hearted attitude. PT was a lot of fun in the First Platoon. And Leroy got his first taste of Army leadership.

Some of the cadet candidates came directly from Army Basic Training and had no service experience. Even as hard-ass Leroy Webb, he was one of those who helped the newbies to adapt. Just as he had done as a young kid, as a high school leader, and at Occidental, he was always tuned in to those around him and would respond to their needs in any way he could. (He still does.)

One aspect of the Prep School routine was NOT anything like West Point: the weekend. At USMAPS, the troops were on their own after Friday PT until assembly at 1630 hours Sunday afternoon. Fort Belvoir was an open Post and US Highway 1 ran North and South through it. A bus stop was three blocks from the Prep School, and the ride was only 30 minutes to the 14th Street Bridge in DC.

The first weekend, Webb, Blumhardt, Ellis, and two other young men took the bus and were dropped off near the Washington Monument. They passed the Monument, the Lincoln Memorial, crossed the bridge, and entered Arlington National Cemetery (ANC). Then, they walked up the hill to the Tomb of The Unknown Soldier. They sat on the benches to watch the Changing of the Guard Ceremony. As the Ceremony began, the Sergeant asked the visitors to stand up. All did except for five or six college-age boys. It seems they were ignorant of protocol (not intentionally being disrespectful). One of the guards went from Shoulder Arms to Port Arms, faced the boys, and said (forcibly), "You will stand up." And they did. Ernie was already learning patriotism and military leadership.

A favorite event was the occasional social dance at the Belvoir Community Center attended by girls from Mary Washington University in Fredericksburg, Virginia. A few cadet candidates met their future wives there. But the lure of downtown DC was even stronger.

In mid-September, a friend of Jim Ellis's dad had business in DC and drove Jim's car to Belvoir, leaving it for Jim to use on weekends. Access to the car opened up a wider range of activities. One rule: any coins in a passenger's pocket went into the government sock hanging from the rearview mirror. Soldiers were paid once a month and had enough money for about 10 days of fun. After that, gas in the car kept the Prep School troops mobile to visit the young ladies that they met every weekend. Their new companions came to DC from all over the country for work experience. Every Senator and Congressman maintained a staff in the District to do all the day-to-day stuff. Who would they hire? Young people, mainly the relatives of their loyal supporters back home, that's who. A "target rich" environment.

In the 1950s there was no Class 6 (liquor) store on an Army post. Only Officer's Clubs and NCO Clubs could sell bottled alcohol and six-packs of beer. Webb and his buddies felt fortunate that Jim was a Corporal (E4), which qualified him for NCO Club membership. Friday at 1630 was set for club shopping. Webb, Blumhardt, Jim, and others would head for DC, prepared for good times. Those good times could sometimes become pretty rowdy. The guys soon learned that Leroy Webb enjoyed creating disruptions now and then. As Jim put it: "He was occasionally confrontational." That was putting it mildly.

The guys didn't know where all that rowdiness came from, maybe it was the tattoo. During his Airborne time, Leroy got tattooed on his lower right arm: "US Paratrooper." There weren't a lot of tattoos in the Army at that time, it was a Navy thing. If you had one on your forearm, it would typically be an anchor, like Popeye's, not a set of jump wings. Leroy's ink was in plain sight, hard not to notice, and likely to be offensive to the swabbies. Just what he wanted.

Leroy was familiar with Anacostia Naval Base in DC. One Friday, he and Jim and a couple of other guys went to the Enlisted Club on Post. The Navy club was full of sailors in their white uniforms, all sitting in booths around the walls. The Prep School guys, in civies, sat at a table and each ordered a beer. Ernie got the idea that all those white uniforms reminded him of how all cooks in the mess hall had to wear all white. Leroy got on top of the table and said, "Look at all of these Airborne cooks!"

Jim remembers: "About half of the sailors got up and came at us. Out the door and heading for the car, only one of our guys was unlucky enough to take a right hook in the face."

USMAPS candidates received first-rate training at the Prep School in leadership, physical fitness, and academics, but they still had to pass the West Point Exam to enter the Academy, just like everyone else. That was a tough filter: only 93 of the 200 candidates in the USMAPS Class of 1958 qualified for West Point. Some had dropped out along the way and for others, that final hurdle was just too high. The Prep School training paid off for the successful candidates however; 75 of the 93 pinned on 2LT bars at West Point four years later.

When it came time to report to the Academy on the first of July, 1958, the Prep School troops were ready. Most new cadets were escorted to the Point by nervous parents, sorrowful girlfriends, or they just fell in with other "newbies" that they met along the way. Every June 30th, the nearby Thayer Hotel was jam-packed.

The Prep School guys approached this as just another field challenge. They broke into squads, assembling in various redoubts in North Jersey, ready to advance at first light. The bus ride north gave them plenty of time to go over what they thought they knew about the upcoming reception. When the bus rolled into Highland Falls, Platoon Leader Blumhardt ordered a halt. He had spotted Benny Havens, an Irish bar located a couple hundred yards south of Thayer Gate. For over a hundred years, this pub had inspired a favorite West Point cadet song, "Benny Havens Oh!" Little did he know about the historic significance of Benny Havens, but it looked like a good place for a final reconnaissance. "Everybody out, form up for rations!" The squad enjoyed some corned beef and cabbage, washed down by a few mugs of Guinness, knowing that would be their last beer for some time.

West Point here we come.

Chapter 3

Webb Enters West Point

West Point on the Hudson

About 50 miles north of New York City, on the west side of the Hudson River, a point of land juts out into the river, giving West Point its name. During the Revolutionary War, a fort was built on the bluff overlooking a sharp "S" curve of the river, a very difficult area to maneuver for warships under sail. A huge chain forged nearby was floated across the river to make any invading force even more vulnerable. Because the British strategy during the Revolutionary War was to sail up the Hudson River, cutting the colonies in two, General George Washington considered West Point to be the most important strategic location in America. It is the oldest continuously occupied fort in the United States. The United States Military Academy was founded there in 1802. The New Cadets were aware they were treading on hallowed ground.

Webb had visited West Point once before with several of his USMA Prep School classmates, but this time it was different. Ernie was now joining the Long Gray Line of this hallowed, national institution. He was a very fit twenty-one-year-old, sporting a paratrooper forearm tattoo and a white-side-wall haircut. He was wearing a long-sleeved shirt and trousers and carrying a small suitcase.

His good friends from Prep School called him "Leroy," as had his high school classmates. But at West Point, somehow, he became "Ernie" to many of us. This first name controversy would be settled permanently in his "Firstie" (senior) year by Pat, the love of his life. It would be Ernie.

Ranging in age from 17 to 21, from all walks of life and all kinds of academic backgrounds, 811 young men joined the "Can-Do" Class of 1962. Some came from high school, some from college, and others from the military. One of these men entering West Point already had a baccalaureate degree, and another was a First Lieutenant in the United States Army. All entered at the same level, took the same classes, were paid the same small salary, and would receive a superb four-year education—if they stuck with it. In return, they would incur a commitment to serve their country an additional four years as an officer.

Of these young men, 601 graduated with Bachelor of Science Degrees in Engineering and the gold bars of a Second Lieutenant. (It would be another eighteen years before a woman graduated.)

Webb was as prepared as any for this challenge. Having gone to the Prep School, he had learned how to spit-shine shoes, clean a rifle, march in formation, and withstand the insults and verbal hazing of the upper-class cadre. This was all part of "plebe" (freshman) year. The first two months of West Point are called "Beast Barracks" and the cadets were called "New Cadets."

Ernie recalled, "As a New Cadet, I was careful not to be a know-it-all, but frankly, it was easy and I did pretty well. For instance, I had already memorized a lot of what they called 'Plebe Poop'—a collection of various tidbits about West Point, dating from many years prior and embedded in the historical culture we were joining. We had to memorize and shout out in a thunderous voice a huge amount of arcane information. I still remember the definition of leather.

'If the fresh skin of an animal, cleaned and divested of all hair, fat, and other extraneous matter, be immersed in a dilute solution of tannic acid, a chemical combination ensues; the gelatinous tissue of the skin is converted into a non-putresible substance, impervious to and insoluble in water. This is leather.'"

A squad of New Cadets from the Class of '62 with their Squad Leader

During Beast Barracks, Ernie stood out in the class as one of the top New Cadets. His military background and training and his tremendous athletic ability and physical fitness made him a star.

On one occasion, the New Cadets had to learn how to negotiate a bayonet course. This course consisted of about six dummies simulating enemy soldiers over a 50-yard course. The New Cadets were taught a series of thrusts using a bayonet fixed to an M1 rifle. Two cadets at a time traversed the two-lane course, required to lunge forward with the bayonet, first stabbing the dummy, then withdrawing the bayonet, and then heaving the butt of the rifle upward, catching the chin of the next dummy with a rifle butt stroke. This regimen simulated close combat experienced by Infantrymen in past wars. The cadets were taught to perform these maneuvers to the count of six or eight for each dummy. After striking the dummy, the cadet would pivot and move on to the next dummy. Keeping with what the Army calls "The Spirit of the Bayonet," the New Cadets were instructed to scream bloody murder at each dummy with the intent of making themselves full-out ferocious and thereby scaring their would-be enemy.

The upper-class cadre then staged a "top bayonet competition" for the entire class of '62.

Bob Carroll recalls:

"This was the first time I met Ernie. I was extremely proud of the fact that I ended up being the best with the bayonet in the 1st Platoon [40 New Cadets]of 6th Company. Ernie was selected as the best of the 3rd Platoon. Ernie and I then went head-to-head in a competition for 6th Company, about 125 men. Ernie won. Later, in competition with the other five companies, Ernie won best bayonet in the class. This was a tremendous honor, and it gave Ernie great visibility as a leader in our class.

My personal recollection is that after having gone through this extra competition and after a long day of practicing this strenuous course multiple times, I was just beat! I was so exhausted I almost didn't make it double-timing with my rifle at Port Arms [diagonal] the two miles back to base camp.

Ernie, however, did not seem tired at all. Just smiling."

In addition to being tough as nails, Ernie also had a devilish side. During Beast Barracks, the New Cadets were required to "Double Time" (jog instead of walk) everywhere. But if the New Cadet passed an upperclassman, he was required to return to the "Quick Time" pace (walking naturally). Then, as he passed the upperclassman, he had to render a sharp salute, saying, "Good morning, sir."

Built into this situation was a challenge. While double timing, the New Cadets were required to look nowhere except straight ahead. Yet they were required to spot an upperclassman off to the side, stop, and salute. Often upperclassmen would stop a New Cadet and challenge him for looking around and not keeping his eyes straight ahead. It was really a Catch-22 for the New Cadets. They had to look straight ahead but clearly not miss an upperclassman. Good peripheral vision training!

If the New Cadet was caught looking around, the upperclassman would order him to do 10 repetitions of the "gazing around exercise," which consisted of an eight-count maneuver, thrusting the chin forward, back, to the right, to the center, to the left, and center. Ten repetitions were exhausting.

New Cadet Webb was caught in this dilemma. One upperclassman shouted, "You man, halt! What are you gazing around for? Do you want to buy this place?"

Webb's response could be heard a half mile away. "Yes sir! Got change for a quarter?"

It took about five minutes of three or four upperclassmen screaming at Ernie before he got the grin off his face and his chin plastered back behind his Adam's apple.

After the two months of Beast Barracks, Ernie, Jack Fagan, and Bob Carroll were assigned to A Company, 2nd Regiment, one of 24 companies in the Brigade, which was also called the Corps of Cadets. In Company A2, twenty-eight plebes would join about 75 upperclassmen—in cadet parlance, Sophomores are "Yearlings"; Juniors are "Cows"; and Seniors are "Firsties." They lived together in the barracks, ate together at tables in the mess hall, competed in intermural sports, and went to classes. Very early on, Ernie was recognized by both plebes and upperclassmen as an outstanding leader.

Company A2

1st Row: Art Crowell, Ralph Finelli, Eldon Spradling, TD Culp, Jack Fagan, Dick James
2d Row: Jim Strohmeyer, Bill Evans, Matt Kambrod, Paul Burke, Roger Havercroft, Tom Simcox
3d Row: Skip Holcolm, Joe Gruarino, Ernie Webb, Dick Lembo, Pete King, Barry Thomas
4th Row: Bob Carroll, Fred Tilton, Harry Harris, Erv Kamm, Dick Mayo

The Academy uses a system to assess leadership. It is called "aptitude for the service." It is fundamentally a peer-rating system, whereby both the plebe class and the upper classes rate all the plebes on a ladder from top to bottom. Ernie's aptitude rating was not only the highest among the plebes in A2, it was the highest in the entire class. Because of that, he was awarded a singular honor. When all the upperclassmen, including the First Captain, Brigade Commander, and Heisman Trophy winner Pete Dawkins went home on Christmas leave in 1958, while the plebes were required to remain at The Point, Ernie (then a plebe) was named Acting Brigade Commander.

Ernie recalled, "It was a wonderful time. We had the run of the place. It was kind of like the Academy was left to be run by the mice. Ours was the last class. Starting in 1959 with the class of 1963, plebes were allowed to take Christmas leave."

Ernie's visibility in the class skyrocketed primarily because there is a tradition at West Point for the Brigade Commander from "The Poop Deck" (the balcony of Washington Hall, the cadet mess hall) to call the entire Corps of Cadets to attention for grace before a meal. The First Captain yells, "Battalions Attention!" and he does so with a commanding voice. Ernie performed this function marvelously.

Ernie said, "I did have a pretty loud voice for the mess hall or for commanding a unit at a parade. I recall years later in Germany, at a battalion formation, 700 or so soldiers, the troops could not hear the commands of the Lieutenant Colonel out front. So, they put me, a Second Lieutenant, in the rear of the formation to echo the Colonel's commands. It worked. Yes, I had a pretty good command voice which served me well."

In academics, Ernie was good in the humanities and not so good in the sciences. He often said, "I was the first man in the second half of the class." He would have scored high in humor!

In athletics, Webb was superb. He had always been a fighter, from grade school through high school and on to Prep School. But that was bare knuckles. At West Point, he put on the gloves and won the West Point Welterweight boxing title.

Ernie Webb, West Point Welterweight Champion

He also starred in intramural soccer, lacrosse, and wrestling.

In the final wrestling match for the brigade championship, Ernie was pitted against a good friend and another great leader in the Class of '62, Walter R. Brown.

"If someone was injured, I always went easy on him," Ernie said. "I knew Ron had a bad shoulder from football, and when he winced during the match, I let him up. Because of that, Brown won the match."

Most likely Brown would recall it differently.

By the end of his plebe year at West Point, Ernie was marked as an outstanding leader. Not only did he have a powerful voice, but he was also a force to be reckoned with. He had an engaging personality, a great smile and laugh, healthy self-confidence, great respect for others, and deep loyalty to his friends.

The United States Military Academy is widely considered the premier leadership development institution in the world. The chief focus of its leadership development is on character, with the motto, "Duty, Honor, Country." Ernie fit that mold and starred. With his penchant for a good fight, he embraced these core West Point values, channeled his fierce energy, and continued his track to become a Warrior with a Heart.

His love of country wasn't born at West Point, but it flourished there.

Chapter 4

At War With "The System"

In June of 1959, the plebe year of hazing and extreme restrictions were gone forever for the West Point class of 1962. After finally achieving "Recognition" the day before Graduation Day for the Firsties, the plebes set off for 30 days of leave. This respite was followed by two months of "summer camp" at Camp Buckner, learning how the Army *really* works and getting thoroughly familiar with the weaponry. Ernie's Regular Army training paid off once again.

Webb loading a howitzer

On the outskirts of the West Point Reservation, Camp Buckner was a great change of scenery, where the cadets worked and played hard. It was very physical and tiring, but on the weekends the young ladies arrived and joined the men at formal dances, dressed in evening dresses to parallel the cadets in their starched all-white uniforms. This was a time of transition from "low life" to "top of the world."

When the class returned to West Point and academics, these cadets were true upper-classmen and free at last from the lowly plebe position. Some of those new Yearlings took it out on the new plebes, a kind of payback for what they had gone through. Others simply went wild: sneaking into Highland Falls for beer runs, bringing girlfriends and beer on post for weekend parties, etc., all the stuff that college sophomores do. However, the West Point Tactical Officers, who knew all the tricks, were waiting to pounce on the unwary, doling out demerits, confinement hours, or marching tours to fit the crime.

Despite his earlier unruly nature, Ernie Webb was not one of those revengeful or wild Yearlings. He had established himself as one of the top leaders in the Class of '62, following his appointment as Brigade Commander over plebes at Christmas. He also starred in athletics as a running back on the sprint football team, and as an up-and-coming welterweight in the annual boxing tournament. He was doing well in academics also, approaching "the top of the bottom half of the class," as he put it.

Yearling Year was a long-overdue restart of his college career at Occidental three years earlier, without having to worry about maintaining a scholarship. And, if there were any "smart-ass rich kids" around, they blended well into the general population at the Point. Ernie was on a new track, aiming high and full speed ahead.

Cow Year promised to bring new responsibilities and opportunities: Squad leadership as a Cadet Corporal, and leadership by example on the athletic fields, the gym, and the classroom. Ernie was primed for all that. But, on Labor Day Weekend, before the new academic year began, he was ready for a break in the action. His pal Tom Simcox suggested a quick trip to DC, his home base, where he knew all the local hot spots. Ernie had a better idea: "I know how we can make some quick and easy money. Are you in?" Tom wisely opted out.

The idea was to sell return address labels to the new plebes as they joined their regular companies at the end of the summer. This was a gig that Ernie had learned about in the Army and had figured out how to adapt to West

Point. The offer appealed to one's ego—not that young men appointed to the Academy had any ego—with a postage-pre-paid official West Point mark on it (the franking mark), sending the letter was the fastest way to show off their status. The new plebes were an easy target: "Picture this Mister, your first letter home after you've survived Beast Barracks announces your new home for the next four years, with an Academy franking mark to make it official. How do you like this?"

The new plebes must have liked it a lot because business was brisk. And here was a friendly upperclassman, treating them like a real person, instead of chewing them out for something or other. "I'll take a couple dozen of those, Sir!"

But a few other upperclassmen had observed Ernie's operation and didn't like it at all. The next thing Ernie knew, he was summoned before a trio of Tactical Officers to explain what the heck he thought he was doing. Ernie thought that he was helping others, just as he always did. "I really thought that I was doing those plebes a favor and if I could make a few bucks in the process, why not?" The Tactical Officers disagreed. Ignoring Ernie's rationale, they handed down a major "slug."

The word "slug" is cadet jargon for serious punishment for some major infraction of the rules. It typically entails:

- XX demerits (If a cadet exceeds a certain number in a given year he can be expelled.)
- YY hours on The Area (or punishment tours, marching with rifle, back and forth in the cadet barracks area)
- Several months of confinement (to room, mess hall, gym and class)

Reflecting on his entrepreneurial venture, Ernie recalls, "I can't remember exactly how many hours I got because it was my first time walking The Area."

It wouldn't be his last.

Ernie's first negative encounter with Regulations, United States Corps of Cadets (USCC), was a major disappointment of course, but he felt that he had been treated fairly. To Ernie, this was very important, even as he learned the lesson that you have to pay the piper. He presented his case, and the Tactical Department reviewed the facts, made their decision, and applied the punishment.

Walking The Area at West Point

Ernie served his Confinement, walked his hours and by the spring of Cow Year, was enjoying his freedom again. Springtime is when West Point attracts a good number of visitors: take in a baseball game, watch a Parade, or just enjoy the view up and down the Hudson from Trophy Point. Those visitors sometimes included young ladies who just might be attracted to a Man in Uniform. Seeking out pretty creatures is a longtime West Point tradition. The more erudite call it *"cherchez les femmes."* Cadets meander around the large grassy parade field adjoining the cadet barracks called "The Plain." They employ all of the reconnaissance skills taught in Infantry tactics and hope to make "enemy" contact. We are not certain, but we believe the women, not having received any formal training, are pretty good at this too.

One weekend in May, Ernie formed up a squad of A-2 classmates: roommates Pete King, Bill Steiner and neighbor Tom Simcox, and set off on their Recon Mission around The Plain. It wasn't long before contact was made with a covey of coeds who were probably cruising with the same purpose in mind. And they had their own car, no less! A simple plan was quickly proposed: "If you lovelies drive into Highland Falls, pick up a few six-packs, and meet us back here in an hour or so, we'll guide you on a Field Exercise to a beautiful, secluded place." The area was known by cadets as Flirtation Walk or "Flirty." Proposal accepted.

Ernie swears that "…we just shared a few beers with the girls, it didn't go any further than that. We were hopeful, but no." The party on Flirty was going strong until someone noticed that Sunday Supper Formation was imminent. There were several beers left, which were promptly concealed, and the guys said goodbye to the girls and headed back to Barracks. Tom had snagged a couple of beers, which he shared with his roommate, stashed the empties in the nearest dumpster, and joined A-2 company in formation. Ernie and his roomies must have had more than a few leftover beers to consume because they were running late. With not enough time to locate a dumpster, they tossed the empties into their room wastebasket and sprinted into ranks. Big mistake.

The A-2 Tactical Officer (Tac) at that time was a flinty-eyed major who was always on the prowl with his quill pad (for noting demerits), looking for any violation. According to Tom, the Tac pulled a "spot inspection" of the Supper Formation ranks and, as he later reported, "observed a glassy-eyed appearance of several cadets and detected an odor of alcoholic beverages." Mercy!

The Tac didn't let it go at that but followed up with a room inspection of "certain cadets," and headed for Ernie's room. The Tac found the empties and wrote the three roommates up for "Drinking in Barracks."

Tom remembers attending a mandatory lecture in Thayer Hall immediately after that fateful Last Supper. He was in the next seat when someone informed Ernie that "the Tac wants to see you." They all knew that the jig was up; you didn't have a casual meeting with the Tac on a Sunday night.

The Tac had enough evidence on the three men in Ernie's room, but that wasn't enough. He kept pressing Ernie, demanding to know: "Who else?"

Enter: The West Point Honor Code.

The Honor Code at West Point is revered beyond all else. "A cadet does not lie, cheat, or steal or tolerate anyone who does." The Tac was using the honor system to force Ernie to be truthful and rat on his buddies. He was asking Ernie either to lie, stating "no one else" or to tell the truth, offering other names. Ernie would have nothing to do with that and refused to answer the question.

The outcome of the encounter was that Webb, King, and Steiner received a significant "slug," but no other cadet was punished.

The reprimand was one of the heaviest ever for the Class of '62 : All three received 45 demerits, 80 punishment tours, four months confinement. Ernie said, "In combination with an earlier offense, that pushed me past 100 hours on The Area for sure." The Academy men had a name for that distinction: He was now a member of the "Century Club."

Ernie's roommates shared the misery. Bill Steiner's demerit load soon went over the limit and he left West Point at the end of Cow Year. Pete King somehow kept up with playing Army football by dressing in pads and cleats in his room and using his scant free hours for spring practice. He was later harassed by that same A-2 Tac, who apparently filed a false demerit on Pete. Pete fought back, appealing to the Regimental Commander. By the time Company A-2 re-assembled in the Fall of '61, that Tac was gone.

What was Ernie's perspective on the twin disasters of those two major punishments? He knew that he could forget about achieving any cadet rank as a Firstie (senior). He had been broken back to Private and wouldn't qualify for sergeant stripes until he had served his confinement and walked off all those hours on The Area.

His A-2 classmates were proud of Ernie's leadership and potential to be a top-ranking cadet in the Class. All of that promise was now gone, and Ernie knew that he had let them down. Moreover, Ernie knew that he was in for more trouble down the road. "When you're a multiple offender, you're targeted by those Tacs who have a bias towards 'Guilty as charged!' for any possible violation." Ernie had seen it happen to Bill Steiner. But Ernie was determined to survive the abuse: "I am a paratrooper—I can handle it."

Ernie had always demonstrated high integrity, even as a little kid. "If you screw up, own up to it, and tell the truth." As noted earlier, he also possessed a strong sense of empathy for others, standing up for anyone who needed help that he could offer. And he had just learned the hard way that real leadership demanded self-control; no more following destructive impulses.

Run-ins with the Tactical Officers showed Ernie how a true leader should conduct himself, particularly with those who ranked below. He never forgot how it felt to be considered guilty of some offense before he had a chance to defend himself with facts. And he would never ask someone to implicate others, just to avoid taking responsibility for his own actions. He also believed that the Army should celebrate excellent leadership and not tolerate poor examples. His West Point experience was exposing him to both kinds. These values would guide him throughout his military career and beyond. But, in his current situation, West Point was about to present one more challenge.

West Point cadets leaving Thayer Hall in rain gear

Ernie didn't have much trouble with academics during his first two years at the Point. He more than held his own on the math and science stuff and was a real star when it came to deploying the English language. A-2 Company ranked low in academics in those days, and Ernie and a few others were non-stop busy keeping classmates above the dreaded 2.0, the lowest passing grade point average. Jack Fagan coached Math and Science, and Ernie handled anything that looked like Humanities: English, History, Leadership, etc. They covered the Three Rs: Ernie did 'Readin' and 'Ritin', and Fagan did 'Rithmetic.

But the 3rd year introduced cadets to those Twin Terrors, Mechanics of Solids and Mechanics of Fluids. Without Advanced Calculus to tackle those beasts properly, cadets had to grind through the basic formulas (just as Boyle, Hooke, and others had done when they mapped out the field in the 17th Century). To make those calculations, cadets were equipped with that venerable piece of gear—the slide rule.

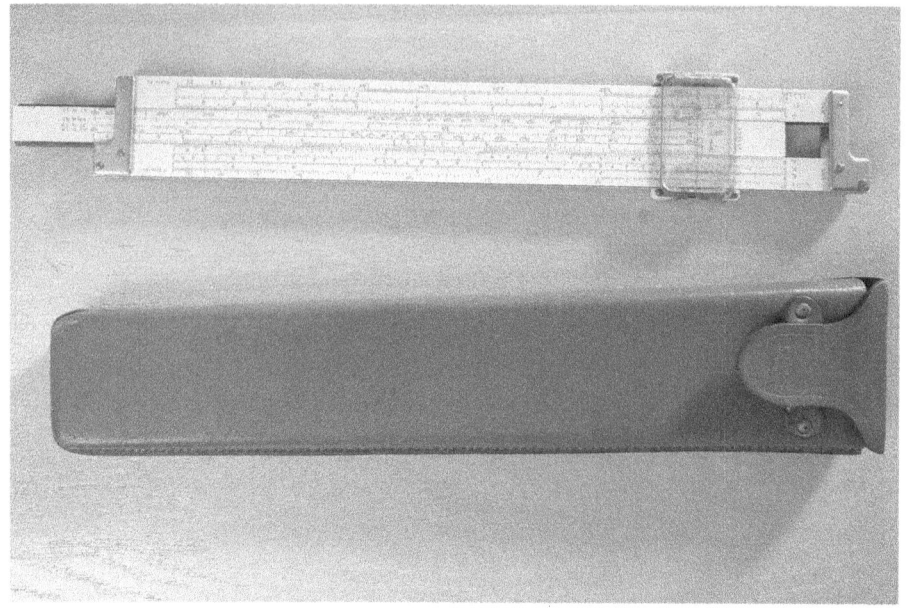

An ancient artifact, the slide rule of Tom Simcox

Somehow, Ernie had fallen below the curve on Fluids and had to nail the End of Semester Exam or get turned out (flunked). His situation probably was the consequence of all the trouble that he was in with USCC, since time spent in service to punishments was time away from studies. But, being the persevering paratrooper that he was, he was determined to "get straightened out." That included academics, so Ernie switched from Offense to Defense under Coach Fagan.

Fagan was prepping for the same test and had figured that the Department was going to lean heavily on the key concept of the Fluids course: the Ideal Gas Law. (PV = nRT, remember?) By swapping dependent and independent variables around, enough problems could be conjured up to populate the whole exam. So, Ernie and Jack worked that equation inside and out, setting up all kinds of possible test problems, throwing in extraneous information here and there, anticipating typical Department shenanigans. It happened just as they had anticipated and they were both victorious. That's an example of a brilliant battle plan, well executed.

Ernie was grateful for the help on specifics but thinks that he might have benefitted as much, if not more, by just hanging around "the smart guys." He talked to a lot of them, not just Fagan.

He learned that the key, as in all West Point exams, was to stay calm, read the problem (RTP), and remember to always fall back on the fundamentals. Not a bad approach for taking exams or preparing for battle (West Point is very good at embedding such discipline into everyday activities.)

Ernie not only aced the exam, he scored higher than Fagan, which bruised Jack's ego a bit—but hey, Mission Accomplished! With that top grade, Ernie would pass Fluids with flying colors, boost his overall GPA, and retain his standing within '62 Can Do.

Not so fast!

You would think that any member of the faculty who is a credible teacher would celebrate the fact that one of his struggling students (like Ernie) finally "got it." In one stroke, that would validate all their hard work in setting up the course, preparing lesson plans, lecturing, managing recitations, grading tests, the whole kit and caboodle. Not this one instructor in the Mechanics of Fluids Department. Ernie was ordered to report to the Department to defend himself against the accusation of cheating on an exam.

Though completely innocent this time, Ernie once again had to face up to accusations of wrongdoing. The instructor had impugned his integrity, and there was no way Ernie was going to stand for that.

If that instructor had suspicions, he could have just opened a discussion: "Great job, Ernie! Frankly, I'm amazed. How did you do that?" Instead, he went "nuclear," declaring a violation of the Cadet Honor Code rather than making any effort to understand the triumph that it was—and he called in the Tactical Officers. Ernie knew that the cheating accusation was motivated, in part, by his recent troubles with USCC. He was a target. "All that other trouble made me a suspect. I was a multiple offender. That's why the Tacs got involved." Ernie also knew the accusation was false, so he was confrontational this time: "It isn't true! Prove it."

They tried to do just that. The Tacs decided to talk to Mechanics of Fluids instructors and cadets in Ernie's class section to determine: "How much does he really know about the subject?" They must have discovered that he knew a lot more than assumed and that he really did ace that exam. The cheating charge was quietly dropped in the Department, and the Cadet Honor Committee was never notified.

Ernie never received any kind of apology from the Tactical Officers, not a word. The Fluids instructor never apologized either, even when the facts came out. But Ernie remembers that there was talk among several academic instructors and some Tactical Officers that he had been mistreated. They were glad that he had prevailed. His classmates certainly felt that way. Ernie's resolve to "stick it out" at the Academy was reinforced by knowing that there were a lot of cadets and officers who had his back.

Ernie took a huge lesson from this episode. "Stick to your guns if you know you are right. And never tolerate or accept authority when that authority is abusive."

He also learned a lesson about the role of teaching. His instructor had forgotten that his job was not to depersonalize and humiliate students but to educate and enlighten them. If the instructor had sought out and discovered the facts for himself, the "cheating" episode would never have happened. Ernie put that lesson into practice every day when he was later assigned to the USMA English Department, and also years later teaching executives and students in the private sector.

Ernie had been at war with the system; both the Tactical Department (The Commandant) and the Academic Department (The Dean). With a lot of time in confinement, which lasted well into Firstie year, Ernie had a lot of time to reflect on lessons learned. He had to think long and hard about continuing his Army career, given the stress, disappointment, and humiliation that almost got him tossed out of the Academy.

His words: "After you've had your ass kicked a couple times, you gain some insight."

He knew that, whatever he did going forward, it was time to make a few course corrections. Above all, "think before you act!" As a young boy, a high school kid, a college freshman, and an Army Pfc, he had acted impulsively far too often, with predictable results. He realized that his current troubles were, for the most part, self-inflicted.

From first-hand experience, he also learned the qualities of Army officers whom he would try to emulate and those whom he would avoid at all costs. He stood up to those officers who harassed him, showing his disrespect for their poor leadership in the process. It wouldn't be the last time that Ernie did exactly that.

But it was time to convert those insights into an Action Plan that made the most sense for him. Ernie was about to experience strong motivation for turning things around.

…And along came Pat.

Chapter 5

The "One and Only"

It was a beautiful afternoon for a walk at West Point, unusually quiet because it was a Saturday when the Army football team was playing an away game at Boston University. Among the cadets confined to the Point that day for various reasons was Ernie Webb. He remembers the exact date, as it was to become part of his destiny: September 30, 1961.

Pat Gilmore, a very attractive 19-year-old woman from Fairlawn, New Jersey, was casually walking around the West Point Plain, the large parade field adjoining the cadet barracks. She had come to the Academy to meet a Yearling, whose name has been lost to history because the blind date didn't work out. Pat decided to stroll The Plain to see if she could meet a different cadet who suited her more. She was dressed in a colorful blouse, an attractive skirt, and walking shoes.

Ernie Webb was taking a different kind of walk. He was "Walking The Area" back and forth, back and forth, for three hours, finishing up his 88 punishment tours for drinking in the barracks some four months earlier. He was dressed in a cadet grey coat (the color from the 1814 Battle of Chippewa). A Firstie private, he wore no stripes because of his discipline difficulties. He had on starched white trousers, the legs of which had to be opened using his dress bayonet. He wore pristine white cotton gloves and a white waist belt with a brass buckle. He was armed with an M1 rifle, not loaded.

Marching back and forth, Ernie spotted Pat who was walking nearby on the sidewalk. They caught each other's eye, and Ernie decided he was going to take a huge chance in order to meet her.

The Officer of the Guard had just inspected the walking formation, and Ernie guessed that the officer would not return for at least 15 minutes. He took the risk of walking off The Area to go over to meet the lovely young lady. It was a high-stakes gamble because he was nearing the maximum allowable number of demerits, over which a cadet could be "found" (kicked out of West Point). Certainly, leaving a formation of Walking The Area would be akin to a soldier leaving his post on guard duty. The consequences would be dire: More demerits could end Ernie's cadet and Army career.

Cadets Walking The Area

So, with rifle in hand, Ernie detoured off The Area to introduce himself. He was suave but quick. He held a very brief conversation with Pat and secured her phone number and a possible date for the next weekend. Somehow, he was able to relate to Pat that his walking tours would be completed by then. Ernie returned to The Area formation of walkers, with a huge smile on his face.

Unbeknown to the above would-be lovers, TD Culp and Bob Carroll, good friends of Ernie's in Company A2, had also been in confinement that weekend. But it was for some smaller infraction that did not warrant "Walking the Area" but did prevent them from leaving their rooms. That same Saturday evening, TD and Bob were very bored and decided to sneak out after Taps and go to the town just off post for a beer. "Taps," with a bell at 23:00 hours, proclaimed that it was time for the cadets to go to sleep. But not these two.

TD and Bob waited for the Cadet in Charge of Quarters (CCQ) to inspect the barracks after Taps. Then the two left in civilian clothes, crossed the barracks area, climbed over the hill, and went through Thayer Gate to visit a bar in Highland Falls called "Benny Havens."

When these two Firsties arrived at Benny Havens Bar, they each downed a bottle of beer. These tasted so good, partly because it was just good ole Budweiser, and partly because it was the forbidden fruit of cadets.

At the time, TD was engaged to Judi–later his wife–and was not interested in the cadet sport of *cherchez les femmes*. Bob, on the other hand, was not just looking for a young lady, but was soon smitten by one at the bar. With the accompaniment of a jukebox, the two of them did a pretty mean jitterbug and a decent cha-cha. Bob was elated to get this girl's name and phone number before he and TD had to hightail it back to the barracks.

The next day was Sunday. As happens at West Point, the 18:00 hour Supper Formation to march to the mess hall is quite somber. It marks the end of the weekend and the beginning of another week of very hard work. It's particularly bad for the plebe (freshmen) class because the plebes must memorize all of that week's information and recite it on call.

At the formation, beyond yelling at the plebes, there were general chatty conversations as the cadets waited for the A2 First Sergeant, Tom Simcox, to command, "Fall in!" Just about everyone was in the usual bad mood.

Uncharacteristically, Bob Carroll ran up to Ernie and exclaimed, "Ernie, you just won't believe it. TD and I snuck out after Taps last night and went to Benny Havens. I met the most fabulous gal. We danced. I got her phone number, and I can't wait to call her and get a date!"

Ernie asked, "What's her name?"

Bob answered, "Pat Gilmore."

"I also got Pat's phone number as she was walking around The Plain yesterday," Ernie said, "and I have a date with her for next weekend. Please don't call her until after I take her out."

Bob was now faced with a serious dilemma. *Should I pursue her now or comply with Ernie's request not to call her for a week?* Bob chose the latter option.

Ernie took Pat out the next weekend and many after that. Bob never called her. Some might say it was the better part of valor.

Ernie always was a lady's man, but Pat was the first woman in his life with whom he truly fell in love. She was gorgeous, smart, outgoing, athletic, very caring, and, like Ernie, a sparkplug. Very soon she became, in cadet vernacular, his "OAO" (One and Only).

While Ernie was at West Point, Pat traveled from New Jersey almost every weekend to see him. She soon met Carol Maluchnik who was dating one of Ernie's best buddies, Jim Ellis. The two North Jersey girls would often travel to West Point together and soon became lifelong friends. Because so many New Jersey girls dated and married the boys in gray, Northern New Jersey was often called the "Mother-In-Law of West Point."

The United States Corps of Cadets on parade circa 1985

Visiting young ladies would watch for their beaus on the parade field every Saturday. Both Pat and Carol were at The Point on one sunny and beautiful Saturday to attend a full Brigade Review for a visiting VIP. The two were part of the very large crowd around the parade field. Brigade Commander and First Captain Jim Ellis stood in front of the reviewing stand and gave the necessary commands to the Corps of Cadets in their unit formations. He would command (loudly), "Bring your units to Attention!" Then, "Bring your units to Present Arms!" And the final order would be, "Pass in Review!"

The commands were loud enough to be heard across the entire Parade Field, certainly a thrill for Jim's proud girlfriend Carol.

The Class of 1962, finishing up a parade

After Ernie's Company, A-2, completed the parade, Ernie and Jim joined the girls. Honestly, Jim thought Carol would be very impressed. However, her first words were, "Don't you ever yell at me like that!" All four had a good laugh.

A week or so later, the two couples were at the First-Class Club. Jim was ready to present to Carol the smaller version of his West Point ring with the crest of the Class of 1962. The West Point class ring tradition dates from the 1840s and has since been adopted by high schools and colleges around the country.

In cadet uniform, Jim was, by regulation, unable to perform the usual "kneel down to present the ring." So, he slid the ring across the table to Carol. Pat later mentioned that she was rather upset that Jim would use this inappropriate method to give a ring to his future wife. Well-attuned to female sensitivities like this, Ernie did not make the same mistake a few months later when he proposed.

Ernie's West Point ring and Pat's miniature

After graduation and Ranger School, Pat and Ernie were married on December 22, 1962, in Fairlawn, New Jersey (the beginning of a beautiful, 58-year marriage).

Lieutenant and Mrs. Ernest Leroy Webb (December, 1962)

In late 1965, Jim and Carol Ellis, now with daughter Tracy, met Ernie and Pat Webb, now with son Mike, in Fayetteville, North Carolina, just outside of Ft. Bragg (now Fort Liberty). The two officers, both captains, were en route to Vietnam.

Together, these brave young women endured the extremely difficult role of a "waiting wife." As shown masterfully in the book and movie, *We Were Soldiers Once, and Young*, the wives of soldiers going to war have a more difficult role in many ways than the men who leave. There is a constant sense of dread for the wife, who tries not to think that a random knock on the front door means that an officer and a chaplain have arrived with terrible news. They know other women who have been informed that their husbands had been killed in action. They know it's a real possibility, and it's terrifying. For Carol, Pat, and other neighborhood waiting wives, an Army sedan showing up was a heart-stopping event. After the sedan visit, the women gathered at the new widow's home to offer support. Such pain!

Pat Webb and Carol Ellis lived that year together in fear. Luckily both men survived.

The two officers ended up a few years later on the faculty at West Point and the two families lived in the same neighborhood.

Carol recalls a party:

"We attended a wonderful costume party, put on by a friend who lived nearby. We had to come as a song title, and the group had to guess the name of the song. Then the individual had to sing it."

Ernie won the prize hands down. He wore black trousers with red and yellow cloth flashing below his belt.

Carol explains, "Goodness Gracious, Great Balls of Fire! Jerry Lee Lewis would have been proud."

Carol and Pat saw each other off and on, mainly at Class of '62 reunions until February 2020, when Jim received a call from Ernie saying that Pat had passed away suddenly and unexpectedly from a heart condition. Carol said goodbye to her close friend of 58 years at the funeral in Pensacola Florida.

In a very reflective mood recently, Ernie said, "I came from humble beginnings and a very difficult family situation with not a lot of love. I trace the fact that I am very emotional back to those days. But that very tough part of my life gave me the lifelong goal of ensuring that my own family had an abundance of love."

Sadly, Pat passed, leaving Ernie with his heart-filled memories. "Pat was the love of my life and my true partner in fulfilling the goal of creating and sustaining a loving family. It all started with Pat, extended to our kids, Mike and Maureen, and culminated with our wonderful grandkids, Makenna and Miller. No lack of love there!"

Love of family and friends is another key marker for the Heart of a Warrior.

And the heart of this warrior belonged to Pat, his "OAO."

Chapter 6

Lieutenant (Ranger) Webb

Webb and the other newly commissioned officers in the Army wore the gold bars of a Second Lieutenant.

Because these Second Lieutenants were fresh out of school and newly minted, Army tradition referred to them as "shave tails" or "butter bars." It took eighteen months for the gold to turn to the silver of a First Lieutenant. More than a few of the Noncommissioned Officers (whose singular job was to train these young officers) believed that the three worst things in the Army were warm beer, wet toilet paper, and Second Lieutenants.

This was not the case for Second Lieutenant Ernest Webb. Unlike many of the butter bars who stepped in straight from college, he had an extensive background as an enlisted man, which served him well not only at the start but also throughout his career as an officer. Plus, he was a great leader.

Second Lieutenant Ernest Webb

After West Point at Fort Benning (now Moore) in Georgia, Webb attended the Infantry Officers Basic Course and then Ranger School. He excelled in both, but he starred in the latter.

Ranger crossing a river

Ranger School is the epitome of warrior training. It allowed Ernie to demonstrate his unbelievable physical endurance and strength and his innate leadership ability in very challenging situations.

One such challenge is best told by Ernie's Ranger Buddy, Don Snider. Not only were Ranger Buddies required to try to throw each other out of a sawdust pit, along with everyone else, to the last man, they also had to assist and support one another to an extraordinary degree.

Rangers in the pit, learning unarmed combat

Don Snider writes:

"First, I need you to understand my own and every West Point graduate's expectations about Ranger School. Simply stated, I knew absolutely I had to succeed, to graduate and earn the coveted Ranger Tab. There was no plan B to me. Being recycled for any reason (failure as Patrol leader, physical exhaustion, or injury most often led ultimately to being dropped from the course) was just not something I could accept.

My Ranger Buddy Ernie Webb was singularly the reason I graduated Ranger School. The explanation is quite simple. During the 'mountain phase' at Camp Dahlonega, while on a very wet, cold, night patrol of endless duration, I tripped on a slippery rock, put out my left arm to catch my fall, and severely dislocated my thumb, the first joint sitting now in the palm of my hand. Patrol stopped, Ranger Instructor diagnosed broken thumb, ordered my evacuation. Medical exam and x-rays confirmed no break. Doctor without passion said it would have been better if it were, he could cast it and I could go on. Instead, he recommended I be recycled because my hand needed surgery to reconstruct, stabilize the thumb joint, followed by a cast for several weeks, therapy, etc.

The doctor had fashioned a metal brace from a long, somewhat flexible strip of aluminum and fit it to my thumb, then taped it to both the wrist and fingers so the thumb was essentially stabilized, immovable, but protected from further damage. I essentially had a 'club' now where I should have had a hand with a thumb opposing four fingers. And, it throbbed, hurt like hell, unceasingly.

The Camp Commander listened to the doctor's recommendation and then asked me, 'Ranger-candidate Snider, what do you want to do?' Likely the best decision I made on Ranger School then came from my cold and quivering lips. 'I want to talk this over with my Buddy, sir.' 'Permission granted.'

After a short discussion of what I could do one-handed over the next week of the mountain phase and three weeks in Florida (like carry such items as a river-crossing rope around my neck/shoulders, but not a machine gun that must be gripped, etc.), Ernie offered the following:

'If you think you can continue, I will do the things you cannot do and get us through the patrols. Our Team will make it.'

In plain language by his self-abnegating acceptance of a huge demand on himself, he was offering me an option to being recycled.

There was no further drama once the decision was made. And by God's grace, no further accidents. I 'clubbed' my way through each patrol and Ernie grunted his way through. So Ranger Team Webb-Snider, after several perilous episodes in the swamps of Florida, were declared Ranger Qualified and graduated on time."

This was Warrior Webb at his finest.

A story from one of our authors, Bob Carroll, demonstrates both Webb's leadership and his sense of humor:

The major tool used in teaching Rangers is the patrol, whereby about 25 men are given a combat mission and tasked to proceed a great distance, mostly at night, through very difficult terrain, without sleep and with little to eat. The Patrol Leader is positioned toward the front of the single file of Rangers, and the Assistant Patrol Leader is near the rear. Rangers are rotated through leadership positions to test and grade their leadership ability.

Webb demonstrated strong leadership on one very difficult and strenuous mission, which Bob was also on. Ernie organized and led a crossing of the raging Yellow River, using ropes in the dark of night, with the temperature in the 20's. A short while later, the Ranger cadre exchanged leadership positions, and Webb went to the rear to be the Assistant Patrol Leader. This happened on the third night of a three-day patrol, a patrol with no sleep.

It is the practice of the Patrol Leader to check periodically to make sure that all of the troops are following him and there are no gaps. He would whisper back, "Pass up the count!" This message was relayed one man at a time all the way back to the rear. It is customary for the man in the rear to start the message going forward by tapping the Ranger in front of him on the butt and count, starting with "one." When the count arrived at the man behind the Patrol Leader, he would state his number; for example, "24." Thus, the Patrol leader would know he had all his Rangers.

After the river crossing (the night still pitch-black), the men were walking through a swamp, where the water surface was just starting to crystallize. One could hear boots cracking through the thin ice that was just starting to freeze. The New Patrol Leader felt it was time to ensure his unit was intact and there was no gap. The word came back to Webb, "Pass up the count." Instead of calling his number ("1"), he stated, "Ernie has to pee."

As this message was whispered forward, you could hear a muffled giggle out of Bob and throughout the ranks. The Patrol Leader got the message not only that all were present, but also that he should halt. He called for a rest break.

Near the back of the single file of men, there happened to be several trees. It was so black you couldn't see them. You had to reach out and feel for them. I reached out my hand and found a tree. Standing, I turned around and leaned my back into it to rest. Ernie could not see me, but he realized a tree was there and proceeded to empty his bladder. It went all over my leg.

In keeping with the required silence, not a word was said.

"I later admitted to Ernie," Bob recalls, "that I was so frozen, all I could think of was how good it felt!"

Ranger wading through the swamp at dusk

After earning the coveted Ranger Tab, the Infantry's mark of a true warrior, Webb was assigned to Company B, 1st Battle Group (Airborne/Mechanized), 505th Parachute Infantry Regiment in Mainz, Germany, at the confluence of the Main and the Rhine Rivers.

Ernie had volunteered for this unit as his first assignment because it was arguably the most prestigious and challenging unit in the Army. All infantrymen have to master the skills and tools of the foot soldier. In addition, the 505th was a mechanized unit, which meant that his unit had to be able to deploy in armored personnel carriers, with the added challenges of maintenance, communication, and greater firepower. Also, this unit was Airborne and had to be able to deploy to the battle by parachute.

The Federal Republic of Germany

Webb loved this challenge and he thrived as a platoon leader over about 40 men. In his first talk with his men, he said, "I'm proud to be a member of this Battalion and this platoon. I'll take care of you…You take care of me." He connected with his troops.

55

Lieutenant Webb and his Non-Commissioned Officers

"I remember we developed a very good reputation," Webb recalls. "We would get the toughest missions. For example, once during a maneuver, we were tasked to go through a very heavily wooded area while the other platoons went around in the farmed fields. On virtually every challenge we came out as the best of the battalion. I remember another platoon leader, who won a particular contest. When it was over, he said, 'I'm not as happy about winning the best platoon in this competition as I am to finally beat Webb's platoon'."

He then became the Company Executive Officer and learned the logistics side of the Army, especially armed personnel carrier maintenance. After a short stint as S3 Air on the battalion staff, he rejoined B Company as Company Commander. Through an army-wide reorganization from Battle Groups to Battalions, B Company was now part of the 2d Battalion (Airborne/Mechanized), 509th Infantry, part of the 8th Infantry Division. He commanded B Company for six months, unusual for a Lieutenant, normally reserved for a Captain.

Webb makes First Lieutenant

*Lieutenant Webb's First Command, B Company, 2nd Battalion,
Airborne / Mechanized 509th Regiment*

After three and a half years as a Lieutenant, Webb had learned the necessary tactical and leadership skills to be a Captain.

Pat assists with Ernie's promotion to Captain, December 1965

Captain Webb with his First Sergeant of B Company, 2nd Battalion, (Airborne/Mechanized) 509th Regiment

There is an old saying in the Army that dates at least to the Civil War: "Go to the sound of the guns." It originally meant that in the chaos of war, go find your buddies, join in, and help them out. You may not see them, but you can hear them.

For Webb, it applied to the fact that there was a war going on. He was superbly trained. That is where he should be.

Warrior, it's time to go to war.

To the sound of the guns.

Vietnam.

Chapter 7

Captain Webb Advising the Vietnamese Airborne

The complex and controversial engagement of the United States in Vietnam dates from the Battle of Dien Bien Phu, March 13 to May 7, 1954. At that disastrous battle, we supported our French allies against the Viet Minh with 80% of the munitions, some by ground and some by air. This was a decisive military defeat that brought an end to French colonial rule in Vietnam and produced the Geneva Accords which split Vietnam in two: the Republic of Vietnam (RVN) in the South and the Democratic Republic of Vietnam (DRV) in the North.

In the late 1950's we sent advisors to assist the RVN military units against the Viet Cong. On February 8, 1962, Military Assistance Command Vietnam (MACV) was formed to coordinate and command all US Forces in Vietnam. On August 7, 1964, the US Congress approved the Gulf of Tonkin Resolution, which authorized President Johnson to deploy troops to Vietnam. In 1965, US Marine and Army units deployed to RVN—by sea and by air. By 1966, the North Vietnamese Army (NVA) had also deployed to the RVN—by foot.

For warriors like Webb, whether or not our nation should deploy forces to a faraway place formerly known as French Indochina was simply not his question to consider. It's a question for the US President as Commander in Chief, as authorized by the US Congress.

Ernie swore an oath to defend the Constitution. That meant to obey any lawful orders from the Commander in Chief as promulgated through the Department of Defense and its robust chain of command that extends down to every soldier, sailor, and airman. For Captain Ernie Webb, this translated to going to war in Vietnam. It wasn't debatable. It was his profession, his mandate, his vow.

En route to Vietnam, he first attended the Military Advisor Training Assistance (MATA) Course at Fort Bragg (now Fort Liberty), North Carolina. Just off-post in Fayetteville, he found a home for Pat and his son Mike to stay in while he was overseas. Close by was Pat's good friend Carol Ellis and daughter Tracy, and that supportive military wives bond helped Ernie and Jim to worry less, as they had to fully step into soldier mode and leave their loved ones.

The MATA course was designed to prepare advisors for their role in helping the Army of the Republic of Vietnam (ARVN). Ernie graduated from this course with a fair capability with the Vietnamese language, but more importantly, a true understanding of the history and culture of the Vietnamese people. Decidedly more than most of his contemporaries in the Army, he had great respect for the Vietnamese and comprehended the nature of the guerrilla war that he would soon be fighting. Unlike most, he understood the infiltration of the population by the VC. He could appreciate that most of the citizens were not communists but just farmers who lived in various villages controlled by communist insurgents.

This fundamental understanding protected him from the virtual cancer that spread throughout the Army during the war. The cancer was the belief that any village occupied by some of the enemy was entirely populated by the VC. This led to some indiscriminate bombing and shooting of populated areas and the killing and maiming of many civilians. The atrocities at My Lai occurred on March 16, 1968, a year after Webb's first tour in Vietnam, but he saw the tendencies. Harm done to civilians indiscriminately caused large swaths of the population to support, rather than repel, the VC guerillas.

This same misunderstanding resulted in some inhumane treatment of prisoners as well as erroneous reporting of dead civilians as enemy killed rather than civilians killed. In focusing on enemy body count, a common statement was, "If he is dead, he is a VC." From the get-go, Ernie rejected this corrupt edict. This served him well on both of his tours in Vietnam.

The full understanding of the above truths is an absolute essential for a Warrior with a Heart!

He joined Airborne Division Advisory Team 162, which consisted of several hundred officers and sergeants advising the Vietnamese Airborne Division, a unit of about 5,000 Vietnamese paratroopers.

Captain Webb was in charge of an advisory team that supported a battalion of about 500 Airborne soldiers. As the advisor to a Vietnamese Lieutenant Colonel, Ernie's role was to advise the Commander and his Operations Officer on battle tactics. He was also the communication link for combat support from the US Army artillery/aviation and the US Air Force. His role kept him close to the battalion headquarters, but he frequently went to battle with the front-line companies.

Captain Webb with Vietnamese Airborne troops

Captain Webb, Senior Advisor to
the 2nd Battalion Vietnamese Airborne Division

Webb's three-man Combat Battalion Advisory Team included a Captain, a Lieutenant, and a Sergeant.

It was a "dream team!"

First Lieutenant then Captain Barry McCaffrey was two years behind Webb at West Point and a very brave and capable officer. His outstanding career included the award of two Distinguished Service Crosses, the promotion to Four-Star General, and the appointment to act as "Drug Czar" under President Clinton. McCaffrey's extraordinary career began under the tutelage of a bona fide warrior named Ernest Webb.

Sergeant First Class Christian "Frenchy" G. Girard was born in France, the son of a French Foreign Legion soldier who had fought near Vinh in French Indo-China (now Vietnam). Frenchy was fearless. On multiple tours in Vietnam, he received three Silver Stars, five Bronze Stars, and two Purple Hearts. After a rough start, he and Webb became very close warrior buddies for an entire year. After Webb left, Frenchy stayed for another year in another unit and sadly was killed.

Captain Barry McCaffrey, Captain Ernie Webb,
and Sergeant First Class Frenchy Girard

Webb's Vietnamese counterpart was Lieutenant Colonel Minh. Ernie thought very highly of Colonel Minh, and the feeling was mutual. According to Webb, the Vietnamese officers, NCOs, and soldiers were outstanding, professional, and brave. When the North Vietnamese overran the country eight years later in 1975, Ernie was relieved to hear that Colonel Minh and his family were able to escape.

Many senior Airborne officers and NCOs were not as lucky. The North Vietnamese instituted a massive indoctrination/imprisonment program for all of the ARVN officers and government officials. Most of the Airborne officers and senior sergeants were thought to be too strong and dedicated to the South and were summarily executed.

The Vietnamese Airborne do not normally give nicknames to the advisors, but in his case, they did. This is how Ernie got one…

His unit was moving across a big valley with a lot of rice paddies, and they got hit by a North Vietnamese battalion that had been tracking them.

The unit froze. Ernie grabbed one of the soldiers and said, "Let's go."

He and the soldier crawled about 75 yards on their bellies in foot-deep water across a rice paddy to the front of six enemy machine guns.

In unison, the two men stood and hurled grenades.

Ernie took out two of the guns with a hand grenade, and the Vietnamese paratrooper got one.

Then Ernie crawled around to a slightly different angle, went forward, and took out the rest of the machine guns. All with grenades!

Word spread throughout the division.

Ernie was a legend.

His nickname became "Co Van Luu Dan" (literally "Advisor Hand Grenade")[2]

---

[2] Ernie describes how he got his nickname, the "Hand Grenade Advisor." Follow the QR code to view a 2-minute video segment.

Or, visit the YouTube channel below and select video #2.
https://www.youtube.com/@the-heart-of-a-warrior

A few days after the hand grenade fight, a Vietnamese officer who was one of the best in the Airborne battalion and a good friend of Ernie's was severely wounded.

Webb tried to get a medevac helicopter to save his life. The American officer in charge of the district in which the battle occurred declined the request for medevac because "the request was not in the proper format."

Two paratroopers

According to Ernie, this man was a coward, a bureaucrat, and the antithesis of a warrior. Furious, Webb's wrath traveled across the airwaves. It is a good thing the two never met. According to the Major, Captain Webb threatened his life.

The helicopter came.

The Major later charged Webb with threatening to kill an officer. Webb didn't deny it. Several of the Major's soldiers who were on the ground with Webb made statements accusing the Major of threatening their own lives.

In the end, all charges were dropped, and the Vietnamese officer survived, although with a significant limp. Years later the incident still infuriated Ernie.[3]

---

[3] Ernie describes what he views as horrible leadership. Follow the QR code to view a 3-minute, 16-second segment.

Or, visit the YouTube channel below and select video #3.
https://www.youtube.com/@the-heart-of-a-warrior

General Westmoreland presents the Silver Star to Captain Webb

In another combat action, Webb's battalion was given the mission to jump into an area that had recently been infested with VC. They picked a drop zone close to a village and adjacent to what was thought to be a major enemy headquarters with an estimated 300 VC. Ernie made the jump from a Vietnamese Air Force C-47. This jump allowed Ernie to wear the coveted star on his master jump wings, indicating that he had jumped in combat. There were many paratroopers who came back from World War II with up to five of these stars for combat jumps, but very few veterans earned it in Vietnam. Another badge of courage for this warrior.

Webb's Master Parachutist Badge with Combat Jump star

Long after retirement, Ernie was reminiscing about his time with Frenchy:

"Frenchy stuttered. I was so frustrated because of not understanding what he was saying that I actually chewed him out one time with language I can't repeat.

Frenchy's response—I remember well. He told me exactly where I could go.

I remember that conversation with great clarity because the next day Frenchy saved my life.

In a battle, I was cut off from any of the Vietnamese soldiers and from Frenchy and McCaffrey. I was partially surrounded by six to eight VC.

Frenchy came to my rescue. No stuttering, just action. He killed several of the enemy and ran the others off. He did this without hesitation or with any concern for his own life. But he saved mine.

We became instant buddies and served together almost a year.

On another tour in Vietnam, Frenchy lost his life."

In Pensacola, Florida, Ernie had a large picture of Frenchy on the wall of his den. It was actually a recruiting poster from a previous assignment at Ft. Bragg (now Ft. Liberty).

One day as Ernie climbed the stairs to his den, Pat told one of his friends, "Ernie's going upstairs to have another cry. Every time he passes that picture on the wall, he tears up. He simply feels that he never adequately thanked this great soldier for what he had done." [4]

War is the only ultimate test for a warrior.

When the bullets are flying, when it's kill or be killed, when you think any day may be your last, when you're physically exhausted, and when you're scared to death, that's when the warrior surfaces and shines.

Ernie stood tall among the Vietnamese Airborne. Ferocious in battle, fearless in leadership. Yet a man of passion and compassion.

A Warrior with a Heart.

---

[4] Ernie describes how Frenchy saved his life. Follow the QR code to view a three-minute segment.

Or, visit the YouTube channel below and select video #4. https://www.youtube.com/@the-heart-of-a-warrior

Chapter 8

Major Webb: A Warrior Goes to War

No thick jungle. No monsoons. No imminent threat of death of your friends or yourself. It would be an understatement to say that Ernie was very happy to be home with his family where the bullets were not flying.

He picked up Pat and Mike in Fayetteville, North Carolina, and headed to Fort Knox, Kentucky, to attend the Armored Officers Advanced Course. This was a nine-month, standard course for captains mid-career. The Knox course was mostly for Armored officers (Tankers), but in the class were Infantry and Field Artillery officers to ensure a combined arms perspective. Ernie was one of those Infantry officers.

The involvement of the US in Vietnam in 1967 was increasing. The deployment of more troop units combined with the individual rotation policy of 12 months required most of the combat arms officers to return for a second tour shortly after their first. In Ernie's case, this would mean that his stay at Fort Knox would be only for one year before returning for his second tour. That year in a relaxed academic environment with family and friends was a needed rest that allowed Ernie to see the birth of his second child, Maureen, on July 17, 1968.

TD Culp, a close friend of the authors and of Ernie from A2 at West Point, did not have that luxury. He was killed in action on September 11, 1967, before his second child, Bob, was born. About fifteen years after the war, Bob and his older brother, TD Jr., visited the river near Cambodia where their father took a fatal round. The two boys arranged to be taken in a small boat to where they heard their father had died. They opened a bottle of Jack Daniels. After a prayer and a toast to their dad, each took a swig and then poured the rest into the Mekong River.

While the Webbs were at Ft. Knox, the country's unrest over the Vietnam War along with the rise of the Black Power movement had captured the nation's attention. Dr. Martin Luther King Jr. was assassinated on April 4, 1968. Robert F Kennedy likewise on June 6, 1968. And the riots in Chicago at the Democrat National Convention occurred in August 1968.

But the Army's focus was on Vietnam. With increased troop strength and a twelve-month individual tour policy, leaders were needed. Ernie Webb received orders for his second tour.

Ernie moved his wife and two children to near Pat's parents' home in New Jersey and had a painful farewell for his second tour. It was on Thanksgiving Day that Ernie boarded a Pan Am jet for Travis Air Base, near San Francisco. The flight was nearly empty, and the frozen dinner of paltry turkey, cranberry sauce, and cold dressing was not mood-enhancing. Homesick already as his tour was just starting, Ernie cried, not for the meal, not for having to go to war, but rather for having to leave his family. He was fearless but wanted no pain for Pat and his children. Not religious, but quite spiritual, he was ready to meet his maker if necessary. A warrior with a heart and soul.

After an overnight in San Francisco, Ernie boarded another charter for Vietnam. He was assigned to the 173rd Airborne Brigade (Separate). This was a 10,000-soldier unit that had been stationed on Okinawa and was the first US Army unit deployed to Vietnam in 1965. All the troops were paratroopers, although the 173rd made only one small (battalion) parachute jump during the entire Vietnam War. Like the other Infantry units during the war, their method of movement was either by helicopter or by foot.

Major Webb joins the 173rd Airborne Brigade (Separate)

Newly promoted Major Webb was assigned to be the Commander of the Jungle School at An Khe where incoming 173rd paratroopers received a week of training before joining their units.

In short order, Ernie Webb transformed a boring, classroom regimen into a condensed Ranger course, truly preparing these paratroopers for the ground combat that awaited them. Ernie later received a letter from a trooper thanking him for teaching him to fight and survive.

It was during this period that Ernie met a very unusual officer who would have a huge impact on his life. Ernie called him "the greatest soldier I ever knew."

Anthony B. Herbert was one of the most decorated Infantrymen in our nation's history. At age 17, he enlisted in the Army, went to jump school, and fought ferociously in Korea, earning three silver stars and four purple hearts (three for bayonet wounds). He was the only American to win the Turkish Government's equivalent of our Medal of Honor. He made Master Sergeant at nineteen. After Korea, he went on a worldwide PR tour for the Army, then received a college education. Herbert added to his warrior legacy as a stand-out commander and instructor in Special Operations and Ranger units.

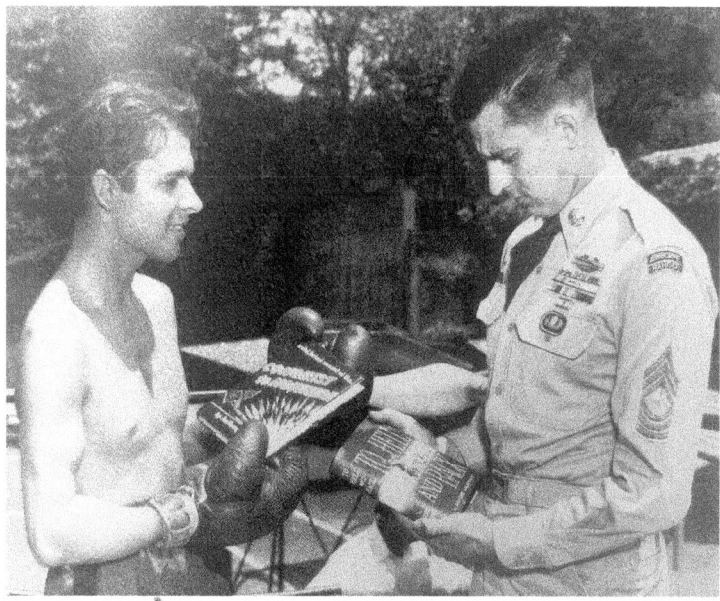

World War II hero Audie Murphy and
Korean War hero Tony Herbert trade stories

Lieutenant Colonel Herbert was assigned to the 173d Brigade as the Inspector General, a role that would prove useful yet foreboding. Useful, in that he would get a good look at the entire organization and its officers as he was preparing to recruit a team for his upcoming battalion command. Foreboding, in that the Inspector General was charged with investigating potential war crimes, and Herbert would later get into a career-ending fight with his bosses, whom he officially charged with refusing to report war crimes.

Herbert had been in Airborne and Ranger units his entire career and knew most of the top sergeants. Joining the 173rd in late 1966 was Master Sergeant Richard L. Childers, whom Herbert knew well. He had been a sergeant in B Company, 1st Airborne Battle Group, 8th Infantry Division in Germany when Captain Herbert commanded the company. On a previous tour in Vietnam, Childers had won a Distinguished Service Cross. When Childers arrived, Herbert had his eye on him and eventually got him assigned to his battalion as "field sergeant major."

What follows can only be called serendipity.

Back in 1963, Second Lieutenant Ernie Webb had joined the same B Company {Redesignated 1st Battalion (Airborne) 509th Infantry} just months after Captain Herbert had left. And guess what? Lieutenant Webb's platoon sergeant was Platoon Sergeant Richard L. Childers.

The tale of how Herbert recruited Webb is best told in his book, *Soldier*. Here is Herbert talking to Childers abour Webb. (Herbert. op. cit. p. 152.)

"Was he any good?"

"Come on, sir, I trained him…He's good, and the brigade needs good men, doesn't it?"

Then over a beer Lieutenant Colonel Herbert teased and coaxed the young Major Webb in words only a true warrior would understand: (ibid. pp. 189-190.)

"Well, old man, how's the famous Jungle School?…You guys training them as well as they trained that lieutenant who radioed his men to open fire on him?" (…The talk around the area was that Ernie had transformed the Jungle School into a worthwhile enterprise. And the Lieutenant gaffe was making the rounds in the 173d.)

"Not a hell of a lot better."

"Tough going?"

"I have a better job offer as a general's aide up at First Field Force Victor."

(I damn near spilled my beer.)

"You're kidding,"

"No, I'm not. I'm not cut out to be a schoolmaster. I came over here to fight."

"No shit."

"The last time I was here I was an advisor. This time I expected to at least have a chance with a US unit."

"And so?"

"And so, I'm leaving."

"Why? Too tough? Or maybe you just can't wait like the rest of us?"

"Tough? Not in this Brigade!"

"So then stay around and help correct it…But if it's too tough, candy-ass, then take off your wings and move out, and when you're a granddaddy, and all the little kiddies sit around and talk about their granddaddy Rangers and paratroopers, yours can say their granddaddy was a general's aide." (He tried to interrupt me, but I wouldn't allow it.) "No, no, just go on, man. Be a general's aide. It's great for the career."

(This was shades of the famous "St. Crispin's Day" or "Band of Brothers" Speech given just prior to the 1415 Battle of Agincourt in Shakespeare's Henry V.)

Herbert later reflected: (ibid. p. 190.)

"We needed all the Ernie Webbs we could get… He was one of the best, just as Master Sergeant Childers had said. He had built a lousy, half-ass, slough-off school into a valuable training device, and he had integrity, guts, and sense. Every last sergeant, whose opinion I cared about said the same about Ernie Webb. He was the best."

On February 4, 1969, Lieutenant Colonel Herbert took command of the 2nd Battalion (Airborne), 503rd Infantry Regiment, 173rd Airborne Brigade (Separate). When he finally got word that Webb was to be his Operations Officer (S3), he was elated: (ibid. p. 203.)

"I [was] so goddamn happy that I actually forgot my Jeep and walked right up the road. … It was a good day. It was a beautiful day. I was getting old Ernie Webb…I would have given my left arm for Ernie, if I had thought that would have brought him to the battalion. I walked along, humming, telling myself to keep quiet about Ernie coming over. Don't tell anybody, Herbert, or like the dumb ass you are, you'll blow it."

The major reason Herbert thought so much of Ernie was that they shared the same warrior philosophy. Bravery was second nature to both, and they both led by example. Going to the front was imperative for a good combat commander.[5]

The two also had the same view about obeying the rules of war with regard to avoiding unnecessary civilian casualties and humanely treating prisoners of war. Ernie gave a powerful speech to new soldiers coming to the battalion about how to treat prisoners of war.[6] In a nutshell, "Treat them as you would like to be treated. See the humanity in the enemy soldiers!"

Herbert and Webb made a great team. They focused on basic Infantry principles, but their application was distinctively different with a style not unlike the Rangers. (ibid. pp.199,200)

- Find'em. Use the battalion reconnaissance platoon for intelligence gathering as opposed to special ambushes; make it the true eyes and ears. Make fast use of intelligence.

- Fix'em. Do not overuse artillery; it is not effective at killing guerilla units that are spread out in hiding or mixed with the population. Use the artillery to fix one flank of the enemy and move around to the rear or to the other flank to engage the enemy. That's real fire and maneuver.

- Fight'em. Attack aggressively by foot using multiple avenues. Train all the companies to execute ranger patrols. Attack often at night. Don't back off and call in Artillery. Close with the enemy as Infantrymen.

- Finish'em. Fight viciously on the ground, to kill the enemy or take prisoners. Put the emphasis on prisoners for their value in intelligence.

---

[5] Ernie explains why he goes to the front as a leader. Follow the QR code to view a 25-second segment.

Or, visit the YouTube channel below and select video #5. https://www.youtube.com/@the-heart-of-a-warrior

---

[6] Ernie demonstrates the Heart of a Warrior in his pitch to newly assigned soldiers. Follow the QR code to view a 1-minute segment.

Or, visit the YouTube channel below and select video #6. https://www.youtube.com/@the-heart-of-a-warrior

The results were quite amazing.

Herbert brags a bit. (ibid. p. 382.)

"We had the highest kill count in the Brigade, the highest prisoner count, the fewest court-martials, the smallest number of accidents, the lowest drug report, the lowest AWOL report, the highest IG inspection report, and the lowest casualty rate. We had lost two men in action since I'd taken command of the battalion, and not a single civilian had died of causes directly attributable to my troops. Yes, that was phenomenal—and of course, it was the result of one hell of a lot of sheer good fortune."

He continues: (ibid. p. 401.)

"Our battalion was aggressive. We accounted for 710 enemy contacts in March 1969, while the other three battalions of the brigade together accounted for only 643."

Webb, in a separate interview, said much the same.

Their essential leadership principle was to lead by example. This put Herbert on the ground with the troops and Webb in a helicopter, or often vice versa. The two officers were equally fearless.

They did not give in to the push for "body count" by senior political and military leadership, which unfortunately encouraged officers to include dead civilians to boost their count of enemy dead. They did everything they could to protect civilians, to report enemy killed correctly, and to report war crimes as required by regulations. They were intensely proud of all their soldiers, especially the way they treated their prisoners of war.[7]

Despite the incredible combat success of the 2/503d, Lieutenant Colonel Herbert was relieved after only 58 days of command. Amazing. The reasons are complex. Herbert maintained that he reported his senior chain of command for covering up war crimes. His bosses reciprocated by implicating Herbert.

---

[7] Ernie talks with pride about his soldiers and their prisoners of war and how they must never lose their humanity. Follow the QR code to view a 1-minute 28-second segment.

Or, visit the YouTube channel below and select video #7.
https://www.youtube.com/@the-heart-of-a-warrior

The chronology is revealing. (ibid. p. 399-402.)

April 2, 1969: Herbert received letters of commendation from the outgoing I Corps Field Forces Vietnam (IFFV) Commander Lieutenant General Peers and his successor Lieutenant General Conners. They were endorsed by his chain of command, Colonel Franklin and Brigadier General Barnes. Herbert was told that he was being recommended for the Distinguished Service Cross. The General said Herbert would get a maximum efficiency report.

April 3, 1969: With that "wind in his sail," Herbert challenged his boss Colonel Franklin with the claim that the chain of command had not responded to reports of war crimes that Herbert had reported weeks earlier.

April 4, 1969: Herbert was relieved of command. Herbert was given one hour to get on a plane to Saigon. When his efficiency report was finalized, General Barnes recommended that Herbert never be allowed to command again. When Webb found out, he told Herbert he was quitting. But Herbert said the troops needed him. Ernie stayed with the 2/503 for another month before taking an aide job with the IFFV Commander.

Herbert left Vietnam and continued to fight this issue after he was back in the States. He made formal charges against his two bosses for covering up war crimes. The two officers were acquitted. Herbert continued to be an outspoken critic, featured in *Life Magazine* and on *The Dick Cavet Show*. February 29, 1972, Herbert finally retired from the Army as a Lieutenant Colonel. At the time, Major Ernie Webb was teaching English at West Point.

Herbert's sidekick and partner, Webb, stood by him during this process and made statements supporting him. While Webb was not a target of the investigation and in the line of fire, the episode left a bad taste in his mouth for the integrity of the Army's senior leadership. Whether that is warranted or not is unclear, but it probably played a role in his decision in 1980 to retire early as a Lieutenant Colonel after twenty years of outstanding service, two as an enlisted man and eighteen as an officer.

Ernie remembers his very short tenure with Herbert as a profound and positive experience. The two were cut out of the same mold. They both demonstrated outstanding bravery and leadership in combat. They respected each other enormously.

Long after his tour with the 173d Airborne Brigade, Ernie recalled two events that he said he will never forget.

The first, according to Webb:

A typical Vietnamese Village,
in this case with the women and children left behind

"The battalion [2/503] was in the process of clearing out the VC from a village. Herbert and I traded off, one on the ground, one in the sky. This time it was my turn to be with the troops with Herbert in a helicopter.

A woman ran up to him and said in Vietnamese, 'There's one still here down that hole. And he's got my baby.'

At least one VC had stayed behind the others and grabbed her one-year-old baby as a hostage.

I went over to the square hole, which measured about two feet by two feet, then dropped down about three feet, then extended horizontally, another six or eight feet. It was really a small tunnel and could probably hold several soldiers.

I approached the edge of the hole and hollered in my pidgin Vietnamese, 'Give us the baby or I'll come down and kill you.'

In Vietnamese, the VC said, 'Go … yourself.'

'Now listen, we got to work here on this. One of us is going to die…you or me…there is no need to involve the baby!'

Again, 'Go … yourself.'

A minute later, the baby was thrown up in the air and the mother caught her. The baby was crying, quite dirty, and wrapped in some kind of towel.

I went back to the hole to try to get the man to come out. The enemy soldier refused. Shots were fired, and I was lucky. I came out unscathed, and the VC was killed.

The woman was overcome with joy and thanked me profusely. She and several other mothers showed us where the VC had booby-trapped some of the paths and huts. Our troops were able to mark the booby traps. As a result, our unit took zero casualties in this engagement." [8]

Many years later, with tears running down his cheeks, Ernie retold this story to a friend and his daughter Maureen:

"I really wish I knew the name of that baby. I'd love to greet that grown person with a very big hug."

His friend: "That baby is about sixty now and may be living in an unknown village somewhere in Communist Vietnam. Probably impossible to find."

His daughter: "Dad, I was telling this story to a Vietnamese-American at my favorite nail salon. I didn't mention if the baby was a boy or girl. In tears, she volunteered to come over to meet you and pretend to be the baby."

The second event, according to Webb:

"We were out on a small ambush patrol. While we were starting to set up, we got hit by about fifteen enemy soldiers. One of my guys was killed. We had to move back. We called in artillery and then went after them.

When we were going through the battle site, cleaning up the area, and looking for the dead and wounded, we came upon this one enemy soldier. His leg had been blown off... It must've been from artillery...

One of the Vietnamese soldiers and I started to. interrogate him. He was a Lieutenant, a platoon leader from North Vietnam. He was going in and out of consciousness. One of my guys showed me his wallet. In it was a picture of his wife and what looked to be a two-year-old baby boy.

---

[8] Ernie tells in greater detail the story of saving a baby. This story proves he is a Warrior with a Heart. Follow the QR code to view a 6-minute segment.

Or, visit the YouTube channel below and select video #8.
https://www.youtube.com/@the-heart-of-a-warrior

Major Webb and fellow soldiers from the 2nd Battalion (Airborne),
503rd Infantry Regiment, 173rd Airborne Brigade (Separate)

Well, my son was going on two....

And I realized again that even though he was the enemy, we're all still humans under God... And I don't want to sound like I'm a religious freak ...but we really all are family.

About this time the guy reaches his hand to hold my hand.

And I held his hand while he died.

Fifty years later, I sometimes wake up in my sleep and look up to see him, his wife, and his baby looking down on me.

That's the kind of thing I remember from Vietnam."[9]

Who can argue that this man is not a Warrior with a Heart?

Next Stop: from the triple canopy jungles of Vietnam to the high-rises on the upper West side of New York—Columbia University.

---

[9] Ernie again shows his humanity with another heart-wrenching war story of a dying enemy officer. Follow the QR code to view a 3-minute segment.

Or, visit the YouTube channel below and select video #9.
https://www.youtube.com/@the-heart-of-a-warrior

Chapter 9

A Warrior with a Pen

The 1968 Democratic National Convention was Ground Zero for the Vietnam anti-war movement. Several prominent universities followed that lead, including Columbia. The Students for a Democratic Society took over the Columbia Administration Building and blocked students and professors from attending class. The anti-war protests across the country continued into 1969. On November 15, 1969, an anti-war demonstration was the largest public protest in US history. The national uproar exploded tragically at Kent State in May of 1970, where the crowd-controlling National Guard left four students shot and killed.

It was during this period that fate would send Major Webb to Columbia for a Master of Arts Degree in English (1969-1971).

Columbia University, Morning Side Heights, New York City

In Vietnam, Ernie "had no idea at all" that he would be assigned to further his education. He was approaching the end of his second tour when the Brigade Staff started to secure follow-on stateside assignments for the short-timers in the officer corps. Ernie was approached by a staff officer who suggested, "What do you think about getting a master's in something and then doing a teaching tour at West Point?"

"Yeah sure, I'll think about it, but I'm a little busy right now."

Ernie was indeed busy preparing for a massive firefight with the VC. A couple of days later, after that action, he did have some time to think about it. His first thoughts reflected on the irony of his situation: "That was a tough fight, and we killed some people. So, one day I'm a hired killer and the next day I'm studying English?"

Ernie didn't really choose English, it chose him. The Staff Officer must have checked Ernie's academic record at the Point, observed that his English Grade Point Average outranked most of his other grades by about a factor of two, and made the call. At that point, Ernie began to realize that the two-for-one academic assignment had some appeal: Pat was living near NYC at the time, surrounded by several institutions of higher learning that offered advanced degrees in English or whatever. He could extend his joyous homecoming, surrounded by family, and further his education in the bargain.

After some research on NYC-area colleges and universities, Ernie discovered that Columbia ranked at or near the top of the list in just about everything. "If I'm going to do this, why not the best?" Moreover, Columbia was an easy commute from where his wife and son were living, was located in a decent community, and was just down the river from West Point, his next duty assignment.

The West Point English Department was fine with Ernie's plan, now it was up to Columbia. Ernie filled out the application, was accepted, and was on his way from Vietnam to the Big Apple.

It didn't take long for Ernie to realize that he was in a hostile environment. Not everyone at Columbia was actively involved in the anti-war protests, but enough of them would show up every day to block other students from attending class, just to get media attention. Two or three of them made the mistake of trying to prevent Ernie from carrying out his mission. He explained to them, "I'm going to class today. You'd better get out of the way." They didn't. "So, I knocked one of these assholes down, broke his nose, got ready for the others, but they backed off."

Columbia University demonstration at the Columbia University Library

The next day, and for a few days after, it was the same story. "I had three or four good fights before the word got out to 'Leave that Army guy alone!'." Many students were understandably intimidated by the protesters, but Ernie never missed a class. Those other students took notice, however, and after a while, some of them approached Ernie to say, "Thanks for what you're doing." It was like high school in Newhall all over again; without even thinking about it, Ernie was protecting the little guy.[10]

When the non-protesting students learned who Ernie was, several of them began to thank Ernie, not just for what he was doing for them at Columbia, but for what he had done for them "over there." They learned about his military record, knew that he was very proud of it, and was not going to tolerate anyone who would "bad-mouth America."

---

[10] Watch and listen to Ernie as he describes his time at Columbia University. Follow the QR code for a 2-minute segment.

Or, visit the YouTube channel below and select video #10.
https://www.youtube.com/@the-heart-of-a-warrior

The hostile environment was still prevalent, but, for Ernie, at least some respect was displayed. "The band didn't play for us soldiers, but there were fewer fights."

Ernie had made it clear that, whatever anyone thought about the war, his core belief was to "protect America!" Ernie sensed that, as time went by, his point of view was accepted, even though he was probably not going to change anyone's mindset. The anti-war protesters learned a lesson: "Don't go there with this guy, unless you're prepared to fight!".

When Ernie was finally able to focus on learning, it was a revelation. The English professors didn't talk about Vietnam at all, despite the anti-war protests in progress all over the campus. They were focused on teaching, whether or not their students were committed to learning. Ernie was committed. After breaking through all that initial hostility, Ernie discovered that he "really enjoyed the rest of it." He earned a Master of Arts Degree with honors in English and American Literature and was accepted for doctoral study.

The Columbia English professors taught the basic rules of writing and Ernie was all-in from the beginning. A bit of irony here perhaps? Ernie had bent or broken all kinds of rules up to that point: in his early life, in high school, in college, as an Army PFC, at West Point, as an Army Officer—every step of the way. But, once learned, he never broke the Rules of Writing. He lived by those rules at Columbia, throughout his Army career, and in his various pursuits thereafter. He still does. He has just about memorized the iconic books *On Writing Well* by William Zinsser and *The Elements of Style* by William Strunk Jr. and E.B. White.

What was a day in the life of an English scholar at Columbia? "They had us writing all kinds of stuff. First you learn the rules, then you apply them over and over. That's the only way that you can hope to teach those rules to someone else." That was the mission that Ernie was determined to accomplish. Ernie's military background permeated much of his writing at Columbia: "You write what you know." But it was important to him that his writing wasn't just dismissed because "…he's a soldier, so what!" Ernie strived to reach a wider audience among his professors and classmates by explaining that his core beliefs applied in a broader context.

Ernie had observed that many Columbia students, even if they weren't active anti-war protestors, were becoming "very anti-American, but they didn't know it. Maybe if they better understood what really happens in wartime situations, I could help to change that attitude." Ernie told the story about how he had rescued a small Vietnamese baby in the middle of a firefight, as a way to demonstrate that basic humanity can be found in the most desperate situations. He told or wrote about that story many times while at Columbia, especially after encounters with the anti-war protestors. "I think that story had more impact at Columbia University than it did in my classes at the Point." The Warrior with a Heart was persuasive, proving that sometimes the pen is at least as mighty as the sword.

Columbia instilled a lifelong love of writing that became a centerpiece of his career from then on. "I'd still be writing if I could." Ernie has always contended that "Columbia got something from me, and I got something from them." That "something" Ernie provided was the respect for another person's point of view, to at least understand it, even if an exchange of beliefs isn't fully achieved. Ernie wasn't leading soldiers into battle at Columbia, but his passion for America and his determination to convey that passion to others was a profound demonstration of his leadership in a much different environment.

After two years, Ernie was ready to take his hard-earned English MA and apply those sacred rules of writing at West Point. The English Department at West Point in 1971 was, as Ernie put it, "old fashioned, run by one tough SOB, who expected his instructors to 'teach the course with the authority and concern as you would in the Army.'" After two years of civilian life, Ernie was back in a Regular Army outfit, "experiencing all the stuff that happens in a good command." He felt right at home.

It turned out that the "tough SOB" Department Head, Colonel Sutherland, was open to new ideas. "Just make your case and I'll take a position on it, one way or the other. I'll consider your idea, maybe even contribute to it, or maybe not. Either way, you'll get a decision." Ernie's "case" was that he wanted to instill the Columbia process for

Major Webb joins the English Department faculty at West Point

writing, with all its strict rules, into the West Point curriculum. Rule-based writing was right in line with the Department authority and concern philosophy, so Ernie got the go-ahead. He was ready to teach writing the way that he had learned it.

There were no anti-war protestors at West Point, but plenty of controversy over the conduct of the Vietnam War. Ernie himself had serious concerns about Army strategy and tactics in Nam, but wouldn't allow that to influence his insistence on "playing by the rules." For him, those rules applied as much to office bull sessions at the Officers Club as to cadets writing term papers. "Anyone is entitled to state a position and defend it. But understand and respect the other guy's position. There are rules about how to talk and how to write, so stick with the process. But don't ever bad-mouth America!"

Ernie's combat record was highly respected at the Point and after a year or two, he was appointed Executive Officer of the Department. That allowed him to extend his teaching approach, that blend of Columbia and West Point, from his classroom to the entire department. His '62 classmates in the department—Don DeSapri, Bill Calhoun, Dick Chegar, and Art Bondshu—were all-in on Ernie's teaching philosophy. Let the revolution begin.

Ernie is still very proud to state that "we probably taught English as well or better than most other institutions." Colonel Sutherland agreed. Some years later, he wrote a recommendation letter for Ernie, including a recollection of their time together at West Point:

> "As a member of the teaching faculty at West Point, Major Webb proved to be a man of boundless energy, imagination, and foresight. By the end of his teaching tour, he had taught both standard and elective courses, served as the Department Executive Officer, and had been promoted to the academic rank of Associate Professor. The latter promotion is most unusual for a non-tenured faculty member. In managing the affairs of the English Department, he proved both affable and outgoing but was nonetheless meticulous about the proper disposition of the institutional responsibilities with which he was charged. I depended upon him heavily in the process of selecting new instructors, arranging their assignments, and supervising their admission to graduate school and their subsequent study."

In addition to his English Department colleagues, about twenty '62 classmates were at West Point serving either as instructors or Tactical Officers. From this group, the following have contributed to this book: Don Snider, Jim Ellis, Bob Carroll, Fred Gordon, and Stan Russell (Citadel '62).

With the help of two of his fellow English instructors, Ernie authored a book in 1974. This happens when you give a pen to a Warrior with a Heart. *The West Point Sketch Book* is a classic collection of "oral traditions" that describes the daily life of cadets over most of the institution's 200 years.

Authors John D. Hart, Ernie Webb, James E. Foley (1974)

West Point Sketch Book, Bicentennial (2004) Edition

There was another dimension to Ernie's leadership of the English Department at West Point that derived from his own cadet experience. From the very beginning, and especially as XO, he made it clear to cadets that they could come to him with any problem. "Before you get your ass in trouble, come talk with me first, because I've been there." Ernie was especially sensitive to cadet uncertainty about cheating, because of the false accusations leveled at him by the Mechanics Department years before.

Ernie knew that, in most cases, cadets weren't trying to cheat, they were just trying to stay out of academic trouble but didn't know where the line was. "You've got to be clear on that. If it looks like cheating, it probably is, so come to me and I'll help you figure it out. All kinds of crap can happen if you don't get yourself clear."

Ernie counseled a lot of cadets during his years at the English Department. He is particularly proud of the personal thanks that he received from one cadet on his Graduation Day: "I couldn't have made it without you."

Ernie eagerly looked forward to his own "graduation" from West Point to the Naval War College (NWC). He viewed that as a logical continuation on his path to becoming a "thinking and writing" warrior. "First you learn the rules, then you teach the rules, then you apply the rules." After Columbia and West Point, he was about to begin the final phase at NWC.

The Naval War College, founded in Newport, Rhode Island, in 1884, serves as a place of original research on all questions relating to war and to the statesmanship connected with war, or the prevention of war. In the 1950s, the curriculum was extended to study all different types of warfare, concentrating on strategy and policy, national security and decision-making, and joint military operations. Ernie was an up-and-coming Army officer sent to the NWC as an exchange student. He was about to expand his thinking and writing from small unit strategy and tactics to a much broader scale. He relished the opportunity.

The NWC faculty wanted Ernie and his fellow soldiers to focus on identifying similarities between the Army and Navy. That would be in keeping with the mission to study joint military operations, but with the "Employment of Naval Forces" as the primary focus. Ernie thought about things differently: "I have a point of view, but it's not just because I'm a soldier." Ernie's interests went beyond the mechanics of conducting warfare to addressing how warfare lessons can be applied to everyday life. "A lot of stuff that we were learning at NWC could be applied more broadly." He only managed a B grade for that Naval Forces assignment but aced all the other courses at NWC and graduated with honors.

Several years later, Ernie was able to put his pen to use for a broader audience. After his battalion command tour in Germany, Ernie was assigned as Managing Editor of *Military Review* (MR), the world's most widely read military journal. This assignment provided the broader audience that he had sought at NWC, including civilian subscribers who were interested in keeping up with military affairs.

Cover of Military Review

After six years in academia (two at Columbia, three at West Point, and one at NWC), it was time for the warrior to get back to soldiers—off to Germany.

Chapter 10

Lieutenant Colonel Webb: Battalion Command

On April 30, 1975, the Webbs, along with the rest of the world, witnessed Americans being sky-lifted from the roof of the American embassy in Saigon, tragically punctuating the end of the war.

In the summer of 1975, Ernie and his family were on orders for Germany.

It had been six years since Ernie had left Vietnam. During that period, he had been immersed in academia (Columbia, West Point, NWC). But it was impossible not to watch the painful end to the war. He realized the acute role the Watergate burglary and scandal played in the debacle.

Here is the chronology:

- June 17, 1972–Watergate
- January 1973–Paris Peace Accords (not impacted by Watergate) promise US troop withdrawal and support if the North attacks
- March 29, 1973–The last American unit leaves Vietnam
- August 9, 1973–Nixon resigns to avoid impeachment
- January 25, 1975–North Vietnam invades the South; President Ford has little political power and the US Congress fails to support South Vietnam
- April 29, 1975–RVN surrenders unconditionally

Ernie's aversion to unethical senior leadership was palpable. Nixon was no exception.

He also realized a basic truth: The spirit, bravery, and tenacity of the warrior will determine the outcome of a battle; but the will, dedication, and strength of the nation will determine the outcome of the war.

This was a depressing time for most warriors who had given so much. It was tragic for the families of the 58,000 who did not make it back. Morale and discipline in the Army were in the pits.

The peacetime Army needed leaders like Webb. It was 10 years—almost to the day—since he had left Mainz, Germany, to return to the States with his wife and two-year-old son Mike.

Now, in 1975, Major (soon to be Lieutenant Colonel) Webb, his wife Pat, twelve-year-old son Mike, and seven-year-old daughter Maureen left Rhode Island for Baumholder, Germany.

The Federal Republic of Germany

Shortly after arriving in Baumholder, Major Webb was tasked with an unusual and difficult assignment. The US Army Kaserne in Baumholder had two Armor (Tank) battalions and three Mechanized Infantry battalions in the Second Brigade of the Eighth Infantry Division. One of the Tank Battalion was in dire straits. After failing almost every test imaginable and then suffering the near mutiny of several officers who abrogated their responsibilities as Company Commanders, the Lieutenant Colonel Commander was relieved. Major Ernie Webb was sent in to turn the battalion around.

This was an unusual assignment for a Major. Very seldom is the command of any battalion-sized unit given to a Major instead of a Lieutenant Colonel. But Ernie's reputation preceded him, and he also had been to the Armor Officers (Tank) Advanced Course, as an Infantry officer. Because of Ernie's background and the delayed arrival of the designated Lieutenant Colonel Tank Battalion Commander, Ernie was picked to take temporary command of the unit with orders to turn it on its head.

He did exactly that. Within several months, the unit was starting to change from one you could not rely on to a strong battalion. The command climate was so bad that Ernie was forced to relieve two Captains commanding companies. He threatened others with Article 15's (nonjudicial command punishment), should they not step up to their responsibilities. The NCOs were eager for strong leadership and responded accordingly. The unit was on the mend when the designated Lieutenant Colonel arrived and took the flag of the Tank Battalion.

Then Ernie's name appeared on the Department of Army battalion command list. Just after he was promoted to Lieutenant Colonel, he was given command of his own Infantry Battalion, the 1st Battalion (Mechanized) 87th Infantry. Because this battalion was in the same brigade at Baumholder, he and his family were not required to move. Also, by then he was acclimated to the area, knew his way around, and had already established a reputation on post as a true leader and warrior.

Ernie recalls what he said to his troops upon assuming command:

"I know this is a good battalion. I know you have good officers and noncommissioned officers, and my only promise to you is to make this a truly powerful fighting machine. I want us to be a team, I want us to be strong, and I want us to be ready for battle. I trust you implicitly. I hope and pray that I can earn your trust as well. We will begin that tomorrow morning at 0800 in a battalion formation for a five-mile run. See you then."

Newly promoted Lieutenant Colonel Webb

1st Battalion (Mechanized) 87th Infantry 8th Infantry Division,
LTC Webb Commanding

See them, he did. And five miles, they ran. What was amazing was that every man in the battalion made it. The main body of about 500 soldiers were in a formation of a column of companies, eight soldiers abreast, with Webb and his Command Sergeant Major in front. The run involved an occasional, slow "airborne shuffle" to catch one's breath, but they ran the entire five miles in just over an hour.

Not everyone kept pace with the main body. There were about fifty stragglers to include a few older NCOs and a Chaplain who could not keep up. Soldiers from each company were tasked to drop back and bring everyone home. With that assistance, the last man shuffled across the finish line about an hour later and was greeted by the entire battalion lined up with Ernie in front, all applauding.

Few had ever run five miles, but they all did that day. And they did it as a team. For the rest of Ernie's command, it would be a weekly event. Ernie set high standards with teamwork being the rallying cry. Every soldier knew that no one would be left behind.

Ernie later said, "The five-mile run was the biggest accomplishment of my battalion command. It brought people together."

About a month into Ernie's command, he was displeased with repeated confrontations between a few soldiers and their NCOs. He took a huge gamble. He orchestrated a battalion event that was unorthodox, dangerous, and powerful.

He had the Sergeant Major form the battalion in a great circle around a pit that had been dug three feet deep and 30 feet across. Then he called out the names of seven men in the battalion who were known to be troublemakers. One had been Court Martialed; another had received an Article 15 punishment; and the others were on every sergeant's problem list. He asked them to jump into the pit.

Then he called out the names of three junior officers and three young NCOs. He asked these six to join him in the pit across from the other seven. Then, in a booming voice, he announced to the entire group. "We have ten minutes in this pit to show who are the tougher men. Stop when you hear the Sergeant Major's whistle."

Then with the cry "LET'S GO!" Ernie launched a full-length headfirst tackle into one of the troublemakers. What ensued was an amazing roughhouse, bodies thrown about, fists swinging, and the entire battalion screaming in delight. The ruckus lasted just 10 minutes, with nobody seeming to win and yet everybody getting a good smack in the face.

After the Sergeant Major's whistle, Ernie spoke, understandably out of breath, "I want everyone in this pit to shake hands and go back to work. The message I want you to remember is that we are all in this together. War is a deadly game. There are no enemies in this battalion. We're all brothers; we are a band of brothers. We have to work together."

The men in the pit shook hands, and the First Sergeants marched the troops back to the barracks shouting a very loud "Jody Cadence," somewhat off-color, befitting the Army culture of the day.

This event pulled together the battalion in a way that nothing else could have. It was creative, gutsy, unorthodox, risky. And in fact, dangerous. No one ever taught this "conflict resolution" technique in any Army leadership class.

But Warrior Webb had extraordinary leadership instincts. He knew what he was doing and succeeded magnificently. Under his command, the unit went on to earn high marks in Inspector General and maintenance inspections as well as the Army Training Tests. His AWOL, Article 15, and drug numbers all went down. The spirit and enthusiasm rose to the skies.

Before this event, Ernie's nickname among the troops was "The Short Little Shit."

After the event, he was called "The Crazy Bastard."

In addition to being daring, Webb also had a wonderful sense of humor.

On one occasion, his battalion in formation was running past a group of school kids. The kids took advantage of the men who had to remain in formation and threw snowballs at the troops. Ernie stopped the battalion. "On my command, let'em fly, but nobody gets hurt." Then 500 men lobbed snowballs at the kids. The kids ran away laughing, and the troops marched back to the barracks.

On another occasion at Ernie's instigation, a parade turned into a very memorable event. A battalion change of command ceremony and parade occurred at Baumholder. At the reviewing stand were the outgoing commander, the incoming commander, and a general officer to officiate the ceremony. The general was an old codger, whose first name happened to be Jeremy and who had a sense of humor—they thought.

Typically, the band leads the five companies of the battalion past the reviewing stand playing a John Philip Sousa march. On this one occasion, however, the band broke out with the song "Jeremiah Was a Bullfrog" (a hit pop song at the time, by the band Three Dog Night). This caused great consternation with the reviewing party and a huge smile on the face of every soldier in the parade. This was not the first or the last time Ernie got crossways with the brass, although his culpability in this little joke was never proven.

The battalion also had a weekly newspaper, which Ernie had a hand in writing. "Every week, rain or shine, we had to put out a newssheet telling stories about soldier and unit successes. We emphasized that leadership responsibilities extended beyond the barracks and should govern their day-to-day lives, especially in a foreign country. 'Never forget that you're representing America in whatever you do.'"

His command tour with the 1/87 completed, Ernie returned to the States.

Ernie had left behind an indelible mark of leadership by example. He received this letter from one of his soldiers:

Lt. Col Ernest l. Webb   *May 1980*

Dear Sir:

First of all, I want to say "Top of the Mountain." I am now sitting here with the April issue of the Army magazine and have just finished reading your article, "The Three Knows of Command." I think it is outstanding. Reading the article brings back to me the outstanding leadership and expertise you showed while commanding the 1/87 Infantry Battalion. Sir, I hope and pray that you and your family are fine.

… I just had to let you know that at least one of your troops respects and loves you for being the outstanding man that you are. I wish you the best in your present job.

Man, we had some times…

Sincerely Yours,

Robert Spradley

Another soldier, J. Flanery, painted and presented to LTC Webb an oil portrait. It hung for decades over the fireplace in his Pensacola home.

A soldier's portrait of Ernie

As a battalion commander in peacetime, Ernie Webb displayed the toughness, grit, creativity, and incredible leadership to earn the nickname "That Crazy Bastard" and prove again that he was truly a Warrior with a Heart.

But soon would come the day when Ernie decided to leave the Army.

What does a warrior do when he goes civilian?

Chapter 11

The Warrior Goes Civilian

It was a tough decision to leave the Army that he loved so much and had served so well.

Ernie has never fully explained why he chose retirement at a time when further career advancement was highly probable. His sterling combat record, his academic credentials, and his outstanding service as a Battalion Commander in the 8th Infantry Division surely marked Ernie for higher rank.

His final assignment as Editor of the *Military Review* in 1978 was disappointing to him in several respects, which may have been a contributing factor. Ernie never fully achieved his goal of elevating the magazine to a broader readership. Also, he insisted that the publication focus on crucial issues confronting the Army, especially leadership quality. Ernie was becoming increasingly concerned about the rise of "political" leadership in the Army, where attention to troop readiness was being sacrificed to career advancement. "Managing up, not down," as he put it. Ernie ensured that the *Military Review* was not going to be used as a vehicle for career promotion at the expense of more thoughtful articles. No "puff pieces" on his watch. Ernie was apparently encountering lots of resistance. A2 classmate Tom Simcox visited Ernie at Fort Leavenworth at this time and noted his dissatisfaction.

Or possibly the main factor was something he had run into before: Ernie respected authority but was never one to kowtow to a high-ranking officer. While he was Editor in Chief of *MR*, he wrote a feature article on leadership. He made the tactical error of including a quote from the Chief of Staff of the Army, a four-star general, but not asking for a quote from the Commandant of The United States Army Command and General Staff College, a three-star with overwatch of *MR*. Lesson: Even the almighty have egos. The article did not sit well with his boss, a Lieutenant General.

Ernie had been rankled for many years about the forced retirement of his boss in Vietnam, Tony Herbert. Herbert's public accusations of war crimes had been vigorously attacked by the Army and its allies, resulting in a defamation lawsuit that reached all the way to the US Supreme Court. As we noted in an earlier chapter, Ernie was Herbert's right-hand-man during those war years and knew the truth of the matter.

The late 1970s and early 1980s were also critical years for the Webb family; Maureen and Mike were teenagers now and he and Pat wanted to maintain a cohesive family unit as the kids grew into adulthood.

But probably the driving force was Pat—who *was* a driving force! She had lived alone through two demanding combat tours her hero husband had survived—barely. She didn't want another.

Ernie and Pat (1978)

So our Warrior with a Heart retired on September 30, 1980, as a Lieutenant Colonel. He had served two years of enlisted time and eighteen years as an officer, thus qualifying him for the 20-year retirement package (50% of base pay with annual cost-of-living raises). He was one of the first from West Point's Class of '62 to retire.

Changing jobs in mid-life can be stressful for anyone, especially if you're a soldier. The military discipline, the camaraderie of Army life, the pride of serving your nation, the assurance that there will be a place for you in that vast organization—all of that is suddenly gone.

United Services Planning Association (USPA), founded in 1958, was well-known within the Army due to its unique focus on saving and investment planning for military families. No other financial services companies were doing that at the time. When USPA established the Independent Research Agency (IRA) in the 60s, their business base within the military really took off. The company added insurance to its savings and investment offerings and began marketing to not only officers, but NCOs, recruits, and anyone wearing the uniform.

Ernie hired on soon after his retirement. He wouldn't be leading troops into battle anymore, but he would be helping his fellow soldiers, just as he had done throughout his career. USPA was about to witness a master class on how salespeople can immediately connect with potential customers, especially soldiers and NCOs. Ernie's innate energy, integrity, empathy for others, and just plain good-heartedness were a natural fit for USPA.

Ernie shared his good fortune with old friend Stan Russell, a neighbor at both West Point and NWC who was winding down his military career at the Pentagon in the early 80s. Stan had already laid out the parameters for his own retirement, following the advice of one of his Pentagon peers. Then Ernie showed up, describing his new employer as an organization having a clear mission, where you could work independently, with strict performance-based compensation, but "flat" enough to enable interaction with anyone, from bottom to top. Stan saw a perfect match for his own retirement plan and a smooth transition from military life. Stan joined USPA and IRA a couple of years after Ernie. Although assigned to different regions, Ernie near Fort Bragg (now Fort Liberty), Stan farther north, the two friends kept in touch whenever they could.

Ernie was an instant success at USPA. His outgoing nature and ability to listen with empathy for the special needs of military families attracted all kinds of new clients. He earned membership in the Summit Club, an exclusive enclave within the company, reserved for those who exhibited outstanding sales performance and excellent rapport with clients and fellow employees. That high profile tapped Ernie for business development opportunities. The company assigned him to open a new territory in Bee County, Texas, adjacent to the sprawling Navy base in Corpus Christi. But, sometime during that period, Ernie's attitude towards USPA began to change.

The Summit Club accolade elevated Ernie several rungs up the corporate ladder. But he always valued his independence too much to be fully engaged in ladder climbing. Besides, more corporate responsibility would have interfered with a very lucrative side gig.

While selling insurance for USPA, Ernie was also selling stocks and bonds for Edward Jones Investments, a rapidly expanding stock brokerage with offices throughout the Southwest. From all reports, Ernie did very well at Edward Jones, as you might expect from a "natural salesman." The company emphasized direct contact with clients, setting up a network of small, independent offices, many located in small towns and often staffed by a solo stockbroker. That type of organization was made-to-order for Ernie's sales style.

But part-time side gigs don't mix well with full-time insurance sales quotas and Ernie's performance must have started to slide. USPA probably noticed something amiss because Ernie was recalled to North Carolina before completing his Texas assignment. He had maintained his independence, but he was back to selling insurance to the troops in and around Fort Bragg (now Fort Liberty). The ascension of the corporate ladder was on hold indefinitely.

Stan had a get-together with Ernie at Bragg sometime in the mid-eighties and sensed that something was wrong. "Ernie was a little cool towards me, not acting like the friendly, back-slapping, joking guy that I used to know." Stan closed the door to give them privacy. "Ernie, we've been friends for over twenty years. What's up?"

"Well," Ernie said, "I have to be careful, you're one of them now." By "them" Ernie meant "management."

Stan had progressed very nicely in his own career at USPA. He was part of "management" as Manager for the Southeast Region of the company. Stan didn't sense any resentment from Ernie about their divergent paths. It was almost as if Ernie wanted to be part of the management team but couldn't bring himself to do what had to be done to fall in and climb the ladder.

The two old friends patched things up quickly, but Stan knew that things were different.

Shortly after that meeting with Stan Russell at Fort Bragg (now Fort Liberty), Ernie began to realize that something was missing for him in his fast-paced, high-octane career path. Making a lot of money is nice, but if it threatens to weaken your hold on your core values, maybe it isn't worth it. Investment companies preach that they always have the best interests of their clients in mind. But, among insurance salesmen and stockbrokers, there is always a fine line between that noble approach and simply pushing products to improve their personal bottom line. Ernie never crossed that line at USPA or at Edward Jones. Just as at West Point as a cadet and later as an English instructor, he always knew where the line was. But he must have realized that, in that results-oriented environment, he was at risk of crossing over.

For Ernie, his core values are always paramount. Helping others is high on that list. Teaching others to help themselves ranks even higher. But LEADING others to discover their best selves is at the top. Neither USPA nor Edward Jones was the kind of place that enabled the full set of Ernie's core values. Our warrior was ready to return to his roots.

On Labor Day 1985, Ernie departed from the pressure-cooker corporate life and returned to the Southwest. He knew that he needed to keep working but was determined to spend more quality time with the family. Perfect timing. Both Maureen and Mike were approaching those scary teenage years, so Ernie and Pat both had to switch gears.

They decided to open a restaurant. *A WHAT?* That's right, the Sub Shoppe was now open for business. Ernie knew that in order to spend quality time with the family, he had to feed them first. What better way? *Just Do It!*

The venture was a full-on family thing for the next several years: Pat managed the books, the kids helped at the counter, and Ernie was out front with the customers. Like many restaurant ventures, hours were long, profits were small, but the reward was a lot more time for family matters. Maureen remembers one incident where she was very glad that her dad was present and accounted for…

Maureen, a good athlete, joined the basketball team at the local middle school. She did just fine on the court, but the locker room was another story. Some of the other girls took notice of the new kid. It started with teasing, progressed to bullying, then got more physical. Maureen must have taken a punch or two before she finally had enough and reported to Dad.

The former 156 lb. West Point Boxing Champion took over. "Never start a fight, but, if you're in one, you're in it to win it."

Ernie dusted off his knowledge of the "sweet science" of boxing and advised Maureen, "Start with quick jabs to the face, that'll keep 'em off balance. You're a lefty like me, so jab with your right hand. They'll either flail at you with both hands or try to land a right over those jabs. Use your footwork to dance clear and keep up those jabs rat-a-tat-tat. They'll have to cover up high—that'll set you up for that left hook that I taught you. They'll never see it coming."

And they didn't. When Maureen was threatened by a couple of the gals the next day, she took them on one after another and knocked them flat. The other girls took notice and backed off. Maureen reported to her dad that their solution had worked beautifully. "I felt pretty proud of myself," she recalls, "and I could tell Dad was proud of me, too."

By the early 90s, Ernie was able to pause and reflect on all that he had achieved up to then. Not his strongest suit; he had been accustomed to making rapid-fire decisions, then figuring out how to deal with the outcomes. Ready, Fire, Aim. This was different. The Army career was long over; corporate life had served its purpose, and the kids had been successfully launched on their own life journey. It was time to craft a new plan along with Pat, with themselves as the primary focus.

But this was not going to be some kind of Golden Years fadeout. Ernie had way too much left in the tank for that. And he really missed the "good stuff" about the military: camaraderie, devotion to a cause larger than oneself, and the opportunity to LEAD others to a better life. He had always done that with the troops under his command. He didn't know it yet, but he was about to embark on a repeat performance with a whole different audience.

It was fall, 1992, at a reunion at West Point, when a number of old guys from the 1962 "Can-Do" Class were standing around telling their stories, which is what they do. The stories often turned to their sons and daughters to include how great they were all doing.

Ernie chimed in, "At one point in my life, I am sorry to say I really was not there for my son Mike. Maybe it was my career, or maybe I thought Pat could handle him. I didn't realize how much boys need their fathers. You'd think if anyone would be aware of this, it would be me because I had three different dads when I was growing up. But Mike and I were growing apart." His buddies became quiet, listening to their friend sharing from his heart.

"One event hit me like a ton of bricks and drastically changed my viewpoint. It was about eight on a Friday night. Mike had recently gotten his driver's license. He was getting ready to take the car out to meet some friends. I recall Mike had had a bunch of beers and shouldn't be driving. As he passed by Pat and me in the kitchen, he mumbled something like, 'See you in a couple of hours.' I couldn't let him take off in the car. I told him he could not go out. His reply was not appropriate. I caught him in the garage and asked for the keys. He refused, and we had more words." Ernie briefly paused as he put himself back in time and into the scene that still carried pain.

He continued, "He took a swing at me. I pulled back. He missed. And I decked him. He lay on the garage floor crying. I was crying too. I lay down on top of him and told him I could not allow him to go out and kill himself. We spent the night in that unusual position. I think Pat was hiding." Then our Warrior with a Heart finished his story.

"The next morning, we both woke up in the garage, both sober. I told him I loved him. I don't think I had ever said that before. I had been brought up to think that love was a romantic term, not used between kids and parents. My view changed that night. I told him I loved him, and he told me he loved me. I believe that night I was there for him when he needed me."

Bob Carroll said, "Ernie, you crazy bastard. That's a beautiful 'Be Here Now' story. I've been working for a year on mine, and it's not nearly that powerful."

Ernie: "What the heck are you talking about?"

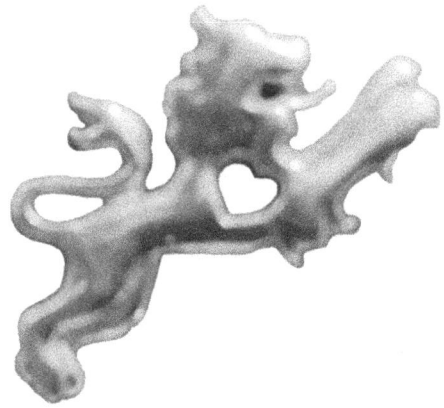

The first logo for the Senn-Delaney Leadership Consulting Group, "Lion with a Heart," fit Webb to a tee.

"About a year ago," Bob explained to his buddies, "I joined The Senn-Delaney Leadership Consulting Group. We consult with Fortune 500 companies who wish to improve their senior-level leadership. Let me tell you how the 'Be Here Now' story fits in.

General Norman Schwarzkopf once said: 'Leadership is both competency and character, and if I had to choose one, I would choose character.' He was not just talking about 'good character' traits like honesty and ethics. Character is made up of a handful of values that could include honesty, respect, accountability, openness, being a team player, supporting others, wanting to win, and maybe being a little feisty if called upon. These are all values. And depending on the company or institution, they can be oriented toward what the organization needs.

Senn-Delaney focuses on the values a particular CEO wants to promote and strengthen. For instance, one CEO said, 'I would give anything if all my top VPs and Division Presidents were more accountable for their team's performance instead of taking on a victim mentality and trying to blame others.' We would make that our consulting mission statement.

You and I are well-schooled in leadership but with a focus on principles like 'lead by example' and 'lead from the front.' Learning those principles will improve the competency or skills of a leader. But it wouldn't impact his or her core character or values. The Senn-Delaney approach was different.

In a three-day workshop, a CEO and his executive team will talk to one another in a way that they never have before. The focus is on values—trust, respect, openness, accountability, and teamwork. The Senn-Delaney workshops typically start with a 'Be Here Now' personal story told by the consultant, demonstrating openness, vulnerability, and compassion.

We have a number of modules in the seminar that encourage others to do the same. The result is a major league jump in openness, trust, and teamwork. After three days the team is ready to do anything and wants this openness and mutual support to continue. It's pretty amazing.

Ernie, you just mastered the 'Be Here Now' story! You should join our company."

Ernie did so, within two weeks.

He was perfect for this job. As a facilitator for the senior group, he could capture the attention with his personal charisma, openness, and vulnerability. The executives had confidence and nearly instant trust in him, which would allow the group to tackle any sensitive topic. The one-on-one, small group and full group discussions were open, free-wheeling, and robust. People greatly respected this feisty, confident Warrior with a Heart who possessed such passion and emotion.

Webb conducts a leadership seminar with a group of senior managers

In one workshop, Ernie had the lead facilitator job with a group that had first-level supervisors and members of the local union. The company was in difficult relations with the union, and the union officials had told their members to show up but not participate. The seminar was launched as usual with the group in a semi-circle around Ernie. But what was abnormal was that about 15 union members were sitting against the wall reading newspapers. Ernie called a break and asked the folks in the background to stay. Having come from a blue-collar background and having been an enlisted man with a tattoo, he felt sure that he knew how to talk to these people.

"I know you have grievances with management, and my guess is there is some validity to them. We are not here today to solve those problems. We are here to understand one another. I also know you will each get an awful lot out of this workshop that will help you personally on the job and also with your families. Join in—not because management has asked you, not because I am asking you, but because it will help you. Please get a coffee and join the circle."

They did, and the workshop was a great success. This warrior-turned-leadership instructor had a way with people, enabling him to relate to any group.

Under the Senn-Delaney banner, Ernie worked with numerous clients across the US in diverse industries ranging from nuclear power plants to corporate restaurant businesses. After six years with Senn-Delaney, Ernie and Bob formed their own company, ACTION Leadership, and continued the same kind of consulting work with clients across the US and several overseas.

Among leadership instructors, none was better than "Uncle Ernie." Workshop participants were immediately engaged by his competitiveness and fighting spirit, as well as his love of other people and keen desire to make a difference for them.

The Warrior with a Heart was delighted to help leaders become better leaders. He loved the challenge. He had found a new home to continue his mission.

Chapter 12

Parade Rest

Around 2005, The Action Leadership Group scaled back, agreeing to take on only a few special projects. The team did start a program for managers who were eager to see the Academy and learn about the leadership training developed at West Point. It was a very successful three-day workshop called "Leadership at the Point." This lasted six or seven years.

The road warrior activities were still fun and very rewarding, but also tiring. Ernie and Bob decided to call off the pursuit.

But Ernie was keen to explore opportunities close to his Pensacola, Florida home, where he could enjoy quality family time and still stay active.

Ernie dusted off his West Point academic credentials and landed a position at Pensacola State University, teaching English Literature and Logic. He continued doing that for the next five years.

Of course, he brought his warrior experience to the class. He told his students about his sergeant in Vietnam whom he had judged as ineffective because the man stuttered. Ernie then related how the next day Sergeant "Frenchy" did not stutter but saved his life. By recounting his relationship with Frenchy in Vietnam, he was able to demonstrate how important it is to refrain from making snap judgments about people. "This ability to accept folks as they are and not to prejudge them is absolutely essential."[11]

---

[11] Ernie uses his personal experience from his early encounter with his buddy Frenchy to teach others not to judge too quickly. Activate the QR code for a 2-minute segment.

Or, visit the YouTube channel below and select video #11.
https://www.youtube.com/@the-heart-of-a-warrior

Of all the groups that Ernie had been associated with over his years, the Rangers were on top. The intense training they received, their dedication, and their achievements were unparalleled. It is tough to top the Paratroopers, but Rangers Lead The Way! And if you are an "Airborne Ranger," look out!

Ranger Slide for Life

As recounted in Chapter 6, early in his career Ernie was a star in Ranger School. But as you can see from this photo later in life, "Once a Ranger, always a Ranger!"

When the Rangers scheduled a special ceremony to honor fallen West Point Rangers, Ernie immediately took notice. Under the leadership of the Class of '64, the word went out to assemble at Fort Benning (now Fort Moore) on 15 October 2010 for a ceremony that honored West Point Rangers killed in action from Vietnam to the present.

Ernie with daughter Maureen (2023)

Two hundred twenty-nine Rangers were to be honored that day, including fifteen from '62 Can Do. Thomas Dale (TD) Culp, the beloved heart and soul of Company A-2, was among those "Can Do" honorees. So, Ernie marshaled the troops to attend the memorial ceremony to honor their old comrade.

At Ft Benning (now Fort Moore),
Georgia Memorial Ceremony for TD Culp 2010
L → R. Bob Carroll, Barry Thomas, Bob Culp, Ernie Webb,
Jim McKay, Jack Fagan, Roger Havercroft

Mid-October in Georgia: a beautiful sunny day for such a somber occasion. But the speakers made sure that the focus was a celebration of the lives of those Rangers killed in action and the legacy that they are part of for all time.

The keynote speaker, General Barry McCaffrey, invoked the oath that all West Pointers swear on their first day as members of the Long Gray Line, reminding everyone that giving your life for your country is the highest honor a soldier can achieve. When the USMA Rangers KIA Honor Roll was read, tears flowed freely.

The remembrances about '62, TD, A-2, Vietnam and all the rest had started the night before at the hotel and continued non-stop the next day. During his speech, McCaffrey called out Ernie, his Vietnam Team commander, as a perfect example of what a Ranger should be. That probably jogged Ernie's memory, recalling all the stories from his military career, especially his combat tours as an Advisor to the Vietnamese Airborne. It became a pass-in-review of all of it: his partnership with Frenchy Girard, his service under LTC Herbert, rescuing a Vietnamese baby from that VC-infested village, and so many more poignant stories.

Ernie was especially eloquent when remembering TD Culp, whose son Bob was able to attend the ceremony. TD knew about, but never got the chance to see Bob, who was born after TD was killed. All the A-2 guys chipped in with TD stories, from his days at the Academy, through Infantry, Airborne and Ranger Schools, to Monterey Language School, and on to Vietnam, where TD had given his life.

Ernie had encountered TD in Nam, shortly before his final mission and was able to provide Bob Culp with details about his dad's final days. Bob told Ernie that he and his brother Tom had traveled to Vietnam to the spot on the Mekong River where TD had been overwhelmed by enemy fire. Ernie, along with Tom Simcox and Bob Carroll, have ensured that the Culp brothers are part of the A-2 family.

One other incident at the Ranger Memorial Ceremony illustrates Ernie's compassion for anyone who has suffered unfair abuse or humiliation. Major General Fred Gorden, USMA '62 and an Airborne Ranger, also attended the ceremony. Fred Gorden is the sole Black graduate of the Class of '62 and was appointed the first Black Commandant of the West Point Corps of Cadets in 1987.

Fred, like Ernie and many others in the class, attended Airborne and Ranger Schools at Fort Benning (now Fort Moore) right after graduation.

At the ceremony, Ernie asked Fred what that experience must have been like.

"It was Georgia in 1962, whaddyathink?" He didn't need to elaborate.

Ernie proceeded to apologize for all the instances of racism that Fred must have encountered, and for all that he still endures.

Gorden doesn't need any apologies; his outstanding career in the face of such abuse speaks for itself. And he must have been bemused that Ernie would feel any responsibility for those hardships.

But Fred knew, as most of the Class of '62 knew: "That's just Ernie being Ernie."

*   *   *

Any smart Warrior with a Heart will spend most of his Parade Rest time with grandkids. This was the case for Ernie.

Ernie was overjoyed to play with McKenna and Miller, Maureen and Mike Thorsen's children.

Unfortunately, Ernie's son Mike died in a tragic accident, leaving his wife Jane with no children.

Mike and Jane Webb

So Grandpop's squad consisted of the two little "M and M's," McKenna and Miller. He had commanded hundreds of soldiers but none so special as this squad!

Ernie rated his "unit" top-notch in morale, discipline, and tactical proficiency. According to Ernie, the squad didn't go on long maneuvers, but Ernie spent many hours perfecting the art of building cardboard fortifications. "You never know when you might be attacked by raccoons!" Whenever the squad completed this or that little project, Ernie would confer appropriate awards and badges. Something simple—a sparkly pendant, fashioned out of some leftover aluminum foil or a bright pin-on ribbon, or a cardboard placard with the child's name embossed—anything to make the junior squad member feel special. Anything like that was sorely missing for young Ernie in those hardscrabble pre-war days in Stillwater.

As the kids grew, they continued to see Ernie when he moved into his retirement home.

They do grow up fast, don't they?

Ernie and granddaughter McKenna

It was a good thing the grandkids, as well as Maureen, were close by, because Ernie never recovered from Pat's passing in 2020.

Ernie and Pat, Naples, Florida

After a bad fall while jogging, Ernie moved into Assisted Living in Pensacola in 2021. Daughter Maureen became his Top Sergeant during this interlude. Pain management is a tricky business, and the medics often have to mix and match different strategies to suit the patient's particular situation. Maureen made sure that they were always "on point" and applied "course corrections" whenever necessary. Like her Old Man, Maureen kept the objective in focus at all times; the medical community learned to do the same.

Webb with daughter Maureen, Veterans Day award ceremony (2022)

A veteran's group in Pensacola recently found Ernie. They had read LTC Herbert's vivid account of his Vietnam combat experience and realized that one of the heroes lived right in their Florida panhandle neighborhood. The vets contacted Maureen and arranged an awards ceremony for Ernie on Veterans Day. Ernie could still fit into his old uniform, and displaying that impressive array of medals and combat ribbons, he was the star of the show.

*Webb receives a Veterans Award at
Summer Vista Assisted Living,
Pensacola, Florida (2022)*

Ernie always exhibits leadership, wherever he happens to be. The other residents in his facility look to him to offer "suggestions" on how the staff might improve their services or their menu. And, when it comes to patriotic endeavors, the Old Soldier really takes over. On the 4th of July, Ernie gathered the residents together and led them in a spirited rendition of "God Bless America." That chorus of 30 or 40 voices, led by a very loud and on-key Ernie Webb, raised the roof that day. America was blessed, everyone cried, and the fireworks were set off.

As always, Ernie sets an example. Independence Day should be honored just as he led his current comrades to do, in appreciation, "from the mountains, to the prairies…"

Webb entertaining the ladies

Ernie still is, and always will be, a warrior. At this stage, he's not battling enemy combatants, "management," or anti-war protestors—or even the Assisted Living staff. As everyone eventually does, Ernie is fighting health issues, but with the same indomitable spirit that he has embodied throughout his entire life. For him, it's not really Parade Rest; it's the Spirit of the Bayonet.

Ernie is still great at telling "war stories," but he does so in a way that does not celebrate himself, reciting all his numerous medals and valor decorations—nothing like that at all. There is always an element of humanity that shines through those terrible encounters when his life was on the line.

"I've had many fights, can't remember most of them. Something special has to click for me in order to bring it all back. Like saving that Vietnamese baby. Like Frenchy saving my life. Like the dying VC reaching out his hand to shake mine."

Ernie always finds a way to fit those crises into a broader context, demonstrating that you can be a ferocious warrior, yet still retain your basic values, your integrity, your humanity, and your respect for others, even your enemies.

His patriotism is powerful. He grew up in rough times from a fractured family, but fate took him on an unpredictable ride. We, the authors, salute him as his journey took him through jump school, West Point, serving in Germany, Vietnam (twice), Columbia University, teaching at West Point, and for the Army in Europe—all in exemplary service to his country. He proudly wore his nation's uniform.

According to Ernie, the best gift he ever received was at the Assisted Living facility, when he was presented with a beautiful, expertly folded American flag.

When he received the flag, the old Warrior clutched it to his Heart, his tears flowing.

About the Authors

Bob Carroll graduated with the West Point Class of 1962 and served his nation for twenty-one years, retiring as a Colonel. Having specialized in leadership development in the Army, he applied those skills to teaching leadership and team building to executives in corporate America. Bob and Kathleen hail from Charleston, SC, where they enjoy the arts, dancing, and the exciting game of croquet.

Jim Ellis enlisted in the Army in 1955, graduated from West Point in 1962, and served 32 years as an officer. Combat tours: Dominican Republic, Vietnam (two tours. General Officer assignments: Defense Representative to Pakistan, Commanding General 10th Mountain Division, Commanding General Third Army. Retired as a Lieutenant General. Then, President and Board Chairman of a charity for seriously ill children founded by Paul Newman and General Norman Schwarzkopf. Jim and his wife Carol live in Tampa, Florida, near all their children and grandchildren.

Jack Fagan was honorably discharged from the Army less than a year after his West Point graduation, due to an incurable skin condition. For the next 30 years, he served his country in executive positions for several Department of Defense contractors, a "Cold Warrior," as it were. Jack resides in the Boston area but spends as much time as possible along with his wife Barbara and various kids, grandkids, and cousins, at his getaway camp in the Western Mountains of Maine.

Appendix

How to Use QR Codes

There are QR (Quick Response) square graphic images within this book which allow instant access to relevant video clips on the internet. For those who might find the QR code scanning process unfamiliar, here are detailed instructions:

Lay the book flat on a table and open to the page with the QR code (the black-and-white square image).

Turn on your smartphone and open the camera application.

For iPhone Users: Point your camera at the QR code. A notification should appear as a frame or box around the QR code.

For Android Users: Point your camera at the QR code. If no notification appears, you might need to enable QR code scanning in your camera settings or use a QR scanner app from the Google Play Store.

Position your camera so that the QR code fits within the frame.

A notification will appear on your screen with a link (e.g., "youtube.com").

Tap on the verbal notification to open the video clip on your phone's browser. Within seconds, this will take you to the Webb interview segment.

After watching the clip, you can close the video and turn off your camera.

If you encounter any difficulties, you can easily access each of the 11 video clips, which are hosted on a special YouTube channel.

https://www.youtube.com/@the-heart-of-a-warrior

.

www.ingramcontent.com/pod-product-compliance
Lightning Source LLC
Chambersburg PA
CBHW051533120626
46551CB00012B/1200